Introduction

This issue of the *Cornell Journal of Architecture* is about the now, the ne
the next in architecture, while simultaneously acknowledging that every
future is intrinsically linked to the *existent*, to the present and its attendant past.
At the heart of issue 8: *RE* is the understanding that the creative act itself is
reiterative; that in rethinking, recombining, reshuffling, recycling, and reimagining
aspects of the world around us, we produce work that both belongs to the current
moment and establishes new future trajectories.

In its two uses as a preposition and as a prefix,* *RE* exceeds the mere notion
of repetition. As understood here, *RE* suggests a number of interrelated approaches:
a *response* to an existing condition, a *criticality* of the status quo, and a *dialogue*
between past, present, and future. At a moment when there is no singularity of
cause, nor cohesive reactionary response, this issue establishes a structure that
engages with the host of topics currently being brought to bear on architecture from
both within and without the discipline, and questions the way in which architecture
is produced and criticized today.

Within the seemingly endless possibilities, patterns have emerged from the
inevitable cohesion between recurrent and urgent themes: issues of reuse and
recycling; of criticism and history in the discipline of architecture; of feedback
loops and regression; of dialogue and correspondence; and of the role that
changing technologies have in restructuring the way we think, see, and remember.
These groupings, by turns both parallel and coalescent, reflect the interconnected
strands of technology, history, theory, and intuition that necessarily reinforce each
other in architectural education and practice today.

As promised in the introduction to issue 7, the *Journal* has undergone a
complete renovation. The layout has been rethought by evolving the DNA of the
original journals to better reflect our new location in network time. The introduc-
tions to issues 1 and 2 mention the geographic isolation of Cornell's campus;
with issue 8, we plug into the global network and embrace our centrality on a new
virtual map. This issue reaches out to writers beyond Ithaca, outside the United
States, and, in some cases, beyond the living world.

Through engagement with a broad range of contributors in these pages, the
issue itself necessarily embodies the kind of correspondence implied by our theme.
In this spirit of dialogue, the *Journal* includes not only the contributor's response,
but the question, article, or image that provoked it. A close reading will reveal
complex threads that weave the articles themselves into an expanded dialogue, or
metalogue. We envision this issue to be the beginning of a conversation that will
incite continued responses from you, dear reader, formally through correspondence
with the editors (cornelljournalofarchitecture.cornell.edu), but also informally,
we hope, in your thinking, practice, and writing in the future.

The Editors of the *Cornell Journal of Architecture*

* *RE* has two major uses: (1) meaning with regard
to, as the preposition in contexts such as re: your
letter; and (2) as the prefix indicating return to a
previous condition, as in review, reiterate, resume,
reimagine, react, redo, and so on. Both uses
suggest dialogue, criticism, feedback, and testing
of an existing condition: a text, a building,
a methodology.

RE: 8

Welcome to the 8th issue of the *Cornell Journal of Architecture*. This issue has been tirelessly pursued by its student editors, by its editor-in-chief Caroline O'Donnell, and by its diverse contributors. I want to take this opportunity to thank the editors as well as the Estate of Ruth P. Thomas for making this journal a continued possibility and success.

We live in especially interesting times—times full of promise and jittery anticipation. This issue is regarded as a relaunch after a contemplative rest following number 7, and in this we encounter a number of remarks on resurrection, reiterations, restarts, and reform.

In Chinese culture, 8 is seen as such an auspicious number; so much so that a telephone number in which every digit was an 8 sold for $270,723 in Chengdu. Consider that the last opening ceremony of the Summer Olympics in Beijing began on 8/8/8 at 8 minutes and 8 seconds past 8 p.m. The traditional fireworks had to be discretely preworked digitally in order to satisfy the media with an artificially enhanced natural spectacle, as the polluted hazy sky in reality was not an adequate media canvas.

On the 8th day of a seven-day week, a cyclical new round begins and we can re-look at the creation we have achieved after a brief time of reflection and rest on the Sabbath. We may not yet know how it will play out, but I can recognize the energy and anticipation of the discipline, the urgency in our discourse, and the readiness for another attempt to ensure that it will not become a discursive Blue Monday.

We find ourselves in the not-yet of our disciplinary time, a transitional phase between the mastery of novel design and production technologies and the ability to control and theorize these new techniques. Entirely different challenges—of representation as well as groundbreaking building technologies—are emerging, requiring architects to repeatedly reorient themselves. Our concept of architecture, its craft, mastery, and virtuoso ability, must be recalibrated and revisited.

We must no longer work digitally just because we can—of course we can. The question today is how to provide discipline and discursive control to the vast array of possibilities, speed, and data. It is through the production of work and through its critical reevaluation that our expertise is advanced. We have played all seven notes and a new octave is beginning, a higher one. As the oscillations double, it is still audible to our critical minds and, even if architecture may struggle to retain the ability to express meaning, it does express the values of the society that creates it.

Now with faster-than-ever computation speed (due to a change from one-digit systems of three bits to systems of one-byte groupings of 8 bioctonions), we will no longer be challenged by merely amassing data, but by understanding it conceptually. We will be challenged to keep our processes open and accept a dynamic of unknowns and not-yets in order to navigate these endless territories.

After all, 8, on its side: is infinity.

Dagmar Richter,
Chair, Department of Architecture, Cornell University

Contents

Dear Kazys,

In his surreal and strangely plausible The Buick, *French artist Cédric Delsaux draws from the abounding cultural archive as he conflates the fictional space and time of a galaxy far, far away with the real space and time of a vague and almost equally alien global city. In our increasingly connected and* atemporal *culture, one that routinely re-mixes, re-shuffles, and re-synchronizes, worlds are produced which, in their very untimeliness, manifest the curious historiographic sensibilities of our time. Under pressure from globalization and new technology, we are faced with a condition that you have called "the immediated real," in which we inhabit a present that we configure within the networked media. How does this new network culture both define and react to architecture and popular culture today?*
    —Eds.

The Buick, Cédric Delsaux, from The Dark Lens, Solo
Exhibition, The Empty Quarter Gallery, Dubai, UAE.

Kazys Varnelis

*is a historian and theorist. He is director of the Network Architecture
Lab at Columbia University's Graduate School of Architecture,
Planning, and Preservation. He received his B.S, M.A., and Ph.D. in the
history of architecture and urbanism from Cornell University in 1994.*

History After the End

Network Culture and Atemporality

By the mid-1990s, theorists of postmodernism mourned its impending death.[1]
In architecture, always the leading indicator for postmodernism, historically
eclectic form lost its currency after the MoMA Deconstructivist Architecture show
in 1989, which delivered up modernism as a handful of broken shards, only to

wane rapidly over the course of the 1990s.[2] Theory fared little better. In architecture the decade was marked by the *Any* project, consisting of a series of conferences, books, and a journal, all time-delimited and coming to a predetermined expiration at the millennium. *Assemblage* magazine, the leading academic theoretical journal in the field, also shut down in 2000, the editors declaring it was time for the "end of the end."[3] Outside of architecture, once it became widely accepted in the academy, theory rushed to declare itself obsolete.[4]

Postmodernism is little lamented today. While we can all agree that somewhere along the line it vanished, nobody bothered to note its death and nobody tends the corpse. Contrast this with the Oedipal nature of postmodernism, which even in its very name announced the temporal succession of the modern. Take Fredric Jameson's seminal 1983 essay, "Postmodernism, or the Cultural Logic of Late Capitalism," which begins with the author's observation that the era was filled with a sense that "some radical break or *coupure*" had taken place.[5] In the *Language of Post-Modern Architecture,* Charles Jencks was more precise, declaring, "Happily, it is possible to date the death of Modern Architecture to a precise moment in time": the controlled implosion of Minoru Yamasaki's Pruitt-Igoe housing in St. Louis, Missouri, at 3:32 p.m., on July 15, 1972. For Jencks, the failure of this award-winning social housing project marked the end of the modernist architectural plan's ability to create positive social change.[6]

In proclaiming rupture, the postmodernists repeat a fundamentally modernist move, made most famous by Virginia Woolf's observation that "on or about December 1910 human character changed …"[7] Certainly in part, Woolf was referring to the impact of the show Manet and the Post-Impressionists mounted that year by her friend Roger Fry, but she was also making a wry commentary on how common such punctual visions of rupture were during her day. Whether it was World War I, the Russian Revolution, Pablo Picasso's *Demoiselles D'Avignon,* or Kazimir Malevich's *Black Square* that marked the break, a temporality of rupture was endemic to modernism. Advocates of postmodernism felt compelled to repeat this.

Mission High School, joelaz, Looking into the Past Group, Flickr, CC (http://www.flickr.com/photos/joelaz/3759353933).

As It Is To-Day, Chris Heathcote (http://asitistoday.com/newsagent).

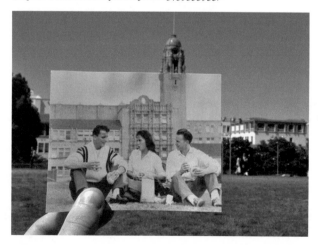

But there is no rupture with postmodernism today, nor are there many claims that our time is somehow different. It's as if the end of history really did come. If anything defines our time, it is science fiction novelist Bruce Sterling's observation that network culture produces a form of historical consciousness marked by atemporality. By this, Sterling means that our desire and our ability to situate ourselves within any kind of broader historical structure have dissipated.[8] The temporal compression caused by globalization and networking technologies, together with an accelerating capitalism, has intensified the ahistorical qualities of modernism and postmodernism, producing an ever more thoroughly atemporal network culture.

Web Services Covers Therapy Overview. Rétro Futurs (http://www.retrofuturs.com).

Unlike modernism and postmodernism, network culture not only refuses to seek legitimation in the past by breaking from previous eras, it fails to even name its own time. Attempts to label the time in a similar fashion: *post-postmodernity, second modernity, altermodernity, digimodernity, liquid modernity,* or *automodernity* all have failed to stick. But we do not even have to look at periodization writ big. Simple chronology trips us up: even now that it has concluded, the last decade remains nameless—is it the 2000s, the '00s, or hinting at emptiness, the "noughties," the "aughts," or worst of all the "naughty aughties"? The lack of a proper name for the decade is no mere product of a linguistic difficulty or a confusion between century, millennium, and decade. Rather, it suggests that we are no longer capable of framing our time.[9]

If we take modernity as a social phenomenon, that is, as the experience of consciously living in a changing present, then we have never been more modern. But, as its reliance on rupture shows, modernity is not merely a timeless sociological category: it is also a period marked by an attitude toward history. To resort to a rather complex construction, modernity is a historiographic concept referring to a period that defined itself by a changed concept of history. Nor is postmodernism different in this respect. It too suggests a supersession, but of modernity, and if it treats history as pastiche—abandoning progress and mocking modernism's teleological goals—the pains it takes to do so underscores that it continues to rely on history for its very existence.[10]

But history is complicated, full of retrogressions and anticipations, projections and false starts. No matter the rhetoric, no period is absolute. Notwithstanding the claim that network culture is ahistorical, it is possible to create a fold in that condition, to understand network culture as a historical process, intensifying premodern, modern, and postmodern temporalities while existing as a unique condition of its own.

keitai, groucho, Flickr, CC (http://www.flickr.com/
photos/groucho/4335685038).

Nevertheless, whereas a historical account of the disappearance of the modern sense of history is a tricky proposition, it is also by no means an epistemological contradiction.[11] Sterling's diagnosis of network culture as atemporal roughly fulfills Jean Baudrillard's 1990s prophecies about the impending end of history. For Baudrillard, if on the one hand, both the contemporary city and information storage technologies produce a hyperdensity, then on the other hand, the omnipresence of the network, the spread of globalization, and with it, the urbanization of the globe lead to a condition of equivocation, of horizontal spread and sameness. Information is simultaneously overdense and overdispersed. This pervasive condition leads to indifference. Baudrillard concludes that our obsession with "real time" information only amplifies this: "if we want immediate enjoyment of the event, if we want to experience it at the instant of its occurrence, as if we were there, this is because we no longer have any confidence in the meaning or purpose of the event."[12] This closure of history marks the onset of an era of *"obscenity,"* governed by "an endless, unbridled proliferation of the social, of the political, of information, of the economic, of the aesthetic, not to mention, of course, the sexual." Media produces an oversaturated condition producing a nothingness, in which concepts can't be formed.[13]

Compelling as Baudrillard's analysis is, it leaves us with little ability to analyze network culture. Our ability to sequence time may be undone, but this does not mean that we cease to exist. As Sterling suggests, network culture is not chaos; it has distinct cultural manifestations produced by the collapse of the past and the future into the present. Network culture's temporality may best be represented by the television show *Lost,* where the temporal sequence of the narrative is undone in a series of flashbacks and flash-forwards. Instead of postmodern hyperspace, we have network culture's hypertime. Or take the *Matrix* trilogy, a product of early network culture that suggests that the present is only a simulation temporally displaced from an impossible future into the past. In novels like *Pattern Recognition, Spook Country,* and *Zero History,* set a year or two before their date of publication, cyberpunk author William Gibson turns away from projecting the future to carefully describing the just-past. Network culture has been marked less by science fiction and more by fantasy in films like *The Lord of the Rings* or *Harry Potter.* But where J.R.R. Tolkien's trilogy was an allegory for total war—remembered in the Second World War and feared in the Cold War—the movie version has nothing to act as an analog for. Instead it serves as a simulation of an alternate reality, temporally out of sequence with ours.

In part, our new attitude toward the past is the product of a change in memory. New technologies make it possible for us to displace our memory into the database. Le Goff observed that electronic memory was "the most spectacular" change of all in the 20th century, allowing research to be performed against vast quantities of historical data. During the last decade, the increase in inexpensive forms of data storage—both in terms of free online email services with high storage quotas and portable hard drives—has made it possible to for us to personally use this calculative faculty. The need to keep track of a particular event becomes unnecessary when it has been recorded in our email program or calendar and can be recalled at a moment's notice. Much as Plato suggested that writing was simultaneously a poison and cure, allowing humans to record information on paper instead of committing it to memory, fast, inexpensive storage makes the past accessible to us even as it undermines our ability to conceptualize it anymore. Why bother to remember the past when we can see it in a proliferation of time-stamped digital images?

More than that, the physical past can also be more easily found today. Until the advent of the global market on the Internet, collecting traces of the past required effort and often threatened failure. Traces of the past hid in used bookstores and antique stores, necessitating that collectors seek out such places. Today, however, the past is readily available for purchase on eBay and other online marketplaces. In turn, generations of historians have scoured the world's archives, emptying them of surprises. The past no longer waits to be discovered and exposed, it becomes subject to the universal exchangeability of capital and the recombinant effects of network culture. This is the past we see in the television show *Mad Men*: a past made up of connoisseurship, a past that matters less for its nostalgic values and more for its thorough perfection, immediately annotated and, as necessary, corrected at websites like the Footnotes of Mad Men.[14]

Under network culture, both the past and the notion of authenticity are revealed as ambiance, as environmental qualities to be experienced. In the fashion industry, for example, the late 1990s and early 2000s were dominated by the supermodernist approach of *haute couture* firms like Prada, Dolce and Gabbana, and Gucci, generally employing new methods and materials to produce clothing designed with performance in mind, but during the later part of the 2000s, fashion turned toward heritage, reviving classic brands like J. Press, Filson, or Pendleton, thereby commodifying tradition as "trad." But unlike the 1980s preppy movement, the heritage turn makes

no claim to class status or to continuity with existing traditions. Rather it marks the
return to American shores of a fascination with Ivy-League-college life that first
emerged in Japan in the 1960s and relies on an obsessive knowledge of vintage
styles, materials, and techniques only possible under network culture.[15] The past has
also been thoroughly rewritten, items re-created with painstaking detail, unfashion-
able flaws removed and cuts improved. Today we can endlessly rewrite the past to
look simultaneously more antique and more appropriate for the present. As we do so,
any lingering traces of earlier temporalities are further extinguished.

　　The result, Bruno Latour writes, is that

> *we have changed time so completely that we have shifted from the time of*
> *Time to the* time of Simultaneity. *Nothing, it seems, accepts to simply*
> *reside in the past, and no one feels intimidated any more by the adjectives*
> *"irrational," "backward" or "archaic." Time, the bygone time of cataclysmic*
> *substitution, has suddenly become something that neither the Left nor the*
> *Right seems to have been fully prepared to encounter: a monstrous time, the*
> *time of cohabitation. Everything has become contemporary.*[16]

Blue House, FAT (Fashion Architecture Taste).

　　Beyond history, our everyday experience of temporality has changed.
Through the net, computers and mobile phones synchronize their time to accurate
servers, establishing a common time with a degree of precision that until recently
was reserved for scientists and the military. But the constant display of time on
computer screens and on mobile phones means that wristwatches are superfluous,
mere fashion accessories. The result has been huge declines in recent sales, the

watch market down 20 percent between 2005 and 2008, as timekeeping functions are absorbed by screens big and small.[17] Still, this new degree of precision belies the looseness that technology makes possible. Modernity was marked by a strict logic of time—embodied first in the pocket watch and then in the wristwatch—and the rise of bureaucratized culture. Timetables and schedules controlled a rationalized temporality that dominated life from the railway station to the home. This is undone today. Technologically, the end of strict timekeeping is made possible by mobile telephony, which eliminates the practical need for precise scheduling. Until its advent, individuals planning to meet each other would have to do so by scheduling meetings at distinct times. Now, individuals can easily make rough plans to meet and then get in touch with each other to coordinate the logistics, even choosing a time and a place while in transit in a common direction. Mobile phones also allow our schedules to soften: when running late, we can contact the other party to advise them. If time used to serve as a mediating device between two parties, mobile telephony allows more efficient continuous and direct contact between them.[18]

This looseness in time serves the increasing demands of capital. The rigid modernist workday is insufficient for a world of constant on-the-go connectivity and globalization. The rigid division between work time and leisure time is long gone as workers now take care of personal tasks and respond to personal emails during work time, even as they are also asked to be always on call, always in touch.[19] A globalized world demands rapid responses during what had previously been off hours, as well as travel back and forth across time zones. Instead of feeling prisoners to an inflexible system, workers are subject to oversaturation.[20] It is hardly any wonder that we lose the ability to sequence.

We observe the anti-temporal nature of network culture in its most distinct literary form, the blog. Organized as a series of time-stamped posts, the newest first, older ones cascading downward in reverse chronological order, blogs appear to have a temporal organization, but this is a ruse. By presenting material in reverse chronological order, blogs undo any potential narrative effect. In practice, it is uncommon to read a blog against the grain, from the oldest posts to the newest. Instead one reads an unfamiliar blog by looking at the most recent post and then, if captivated, scrolls down a bit, rarely making it to the next page. Following a blog means catching it in midstream. Rarely does one scroll back, rather one skims a little off the top and then adds it to an aggregator to follow it along in the future. Past entries, then, act as an archive to direct traffic to the site via search engines.

Blogs are *nonchronous,* in that if there is a sequential relationship between posts on a blog, the precision of the time stamp is meaningless and, in general, bears little relationship to the actual chronological time (the exception being if the blog post corresponds directly to an event—generally a crisis of some sort— taking place in real time). Moreover, even the utility of the sequence is undone by uneven posting practices on different blogs. When one blogger posts much more than another, the latter's older posts may appear newer than the former's, since greater frequency of posting ages older posts more rapidly.[21]

The changes in temporality that mark network culture are not without their effects for politics. When becoming is replaced by being, the possibility of transformation also disappears.[22] But where the reactionary strain in postmodernism stressed a return to family values, today we have left only what Mark Fisher dubs "capitalist realism."[23] This realism eschews the need for legitimation or critique.

It just is, positing no alternative. The critique of industrial society's homogeneity that was common in art under modernism and postmodernism is now absorbed into management theory, the alienated factory worker replaced by the knowledge worker with the "freedom" of job flexibility (which also means no benefits or job security) and the privilege of self-expression as a member of the creative class.[24]

Today's self emerges from the network, not so much a whole individual as a composite entity constituted out of the links it forms with others, a mix of known and unknown others it links to via the net.[25] As its ground, instead of *immediate,* lived experience, the contemporary subject relies on the *immediated* real, a condition in which mediation is a given and life becomes a form of performance, constantly lived in a culture of exposure in exchange for self-affirming feedback.[26] John Tomlinson comes to a similar conclusion about immediacy as the defining condition of 21st-century life. Tomlinson observes that we've become accustomed to instant connection and rapid gratification, and that our economy and work culture not only sustains but constantly accelerates this state. If this is still rather close to the mechanical speed of the moderns, he argues, immediacy also implies proximity, the disappearance of a middle term (Tomlinson observes that the Latin *imme-diatus* means not separated). Under network culture we experience the "'closure of the gap' that has historically separated now from later, here from elsewhere, desire from satisfaction," the gap that was the very aim of modernization to close. Invoking Zygmunt Bauman's idea of a "fluid modernity," Tomlinson posits that the melting of solids is no longer just a stage on the way to a newer condition, but rather an end in itself. Finally, Tomlinson concludes, as I do, that immediacy invokes the powerful role of media in the way we shape our lives. Although these last two terms appear contradictory, he writes, electronic media hide their role in media, seeking to become a seamless part of lived experience.[27]

The collapse of time is tied to the current crisis in capital, which has always relied on temporal progression for its profit model: declining profits in industry since the 1960s coupled with the demands of speculators for accelerating rates of profit. Postmodernity marked not only the end of modernization, it marked the end of the industrial age and, in turn, network culture marked the end of knowledge, work, and the service industries. Like industry, these could not offer enough profit. Instead capital today is dominated by financialization, investment that ideally generates profit with no intermediary commodity. As Jeffrey Nealon suggests, Marx's old model of M-C-M' becomes M-M'.[28] At its highest levels—and these are the levels that dominate the economy—capital is speculative, a game of time given over to ultra-high speed networks. With capital unable to rely on temporal models, it twice experienced crisis. During both the dot.com bubble that marked the start of network culture and the more recent real estate bubble, analysts ran economic models that discounted older data, feeding their models only informa-tion from the recent past, leading to the conclusion that prices of securities or real estate could only go up.[29] Beyond that, capital today turns to new forms of trading that take advantage of the immediate present to extract profits at a speed that no human can process. This high-frequency trading undertaken by investors in possession of massive amounts of capital—mutual funds and other institutional investors but also the megarich—seeking to hide their trades by atomizing them over a short period of time by using software to distribute the trades and make them appear to be a part of the natural trading process. In doing so, such investors hope to mask their investment decisions and take advantage of lower buying and higher trading prices. To take advantage of this, algorithmic traders seek to identify high-frequency trades, buying and selling shares at the expense of the high-frequency traders. All this takes place at the level of milliseconds. With 70 percent of trading now high frequency or algorithmic, the exchange's trading floor becomes obsolete except as theater. No human can participate in such trading once they have given an overall command to buy or sell. Instead, computers talk to computers in data centers located at an intersection of real estate prices and network speed. The fastest algorithms, most-efficient machines, and lowest latency networks win. Time is all-important in trading today but, it is a time that exists that no human can conceive of. We stand at the event-horizon of capital, unable to see past it.[30]

Whether network culture will lead to what Gopal Balakrishnan calls the "stationary state," a protracted condition of a damaged but still dominant capitalism, generating profits at ever higher levels of complexity, whether it might lead to collapse, or whether as Sterling suggests, it will come to an end in a decade or so when we surpass it is as yet unclear.[31] Still, if our goal is to develop a political strategy for network culture or simply to find a way to map it, we need to face up to the temporal condition of the present and go against the grain, instead following Jameson's imperative of dialectical thought to "Always historicize!"[32] For as Neo learns from the Oracle in *Matrix Revolutions,* "everything that has a beginning has an end."

Endnotes

1 Neil Brooks and Josh Toth, *The Mourning After: Attending the Wake of Postmodernism* (New York: Rodopi, 2007), 1; and Peter Osborne, *The Politics of Time: Modernity and Avant-Garde* (New York: Verso, 1995), vii.

2 Hans Ibelings, *Supermodernism: Architecture in the Age of Globalization* (Rotterdam: NAi, 1998). The rapid rise and fall of "Deconstructivist Architecture" inspired the interest in architecture and fashion soon after (personal conversation with Paulette M. Singley). See Paulette Singley and Princeton University School of Architecture, *Architecture: In Fashion* (New York: Princeton Architectural Press, 1994).

3 Compare Jean Baudrillard, *The Illusion of the End* (Stanford, CA: Stanford University Press, 1994) and Hays and Kennedy, "After All, or the End of 'The End of,'" *Assemblage* (2000): 6–7.

4 Michael Payne and John Schad. *Life After Theory* (New York: Continuum, 2003), ix. See also Martin McQuillan, *Post-Theory: New Directions in Criticism* (Edinburgh: Edinburgh University Press, 1999); Thomas Docherty, *After Theory: Postmodernism/ Postmarxism* (New York: Routledge, 1990); and Bruno Latour, "Why Has Critique Run Out of Steam? From Matters of Fact to Matters of Concern," *Critical Inquiry* 30, no. 2 (2004).

5 Fredric Jameson, *Postmodernism, or, the Cultural Logic of Late Capitalism*, Post-Contemporary Interventions (Durham: Duke University Press, 1991), 1.

6 Charles Jencks, *The Language of Post-Modern Architecture* (New York: Rizzoli, 1977), 9.

7 Virginia Woolf, *Mr. Bennett and Mrs. Brown* (London: The Hogarth Press, 1924), 4.

8 Bruce Sterling, "Atemporality for the Creative Artist," in *Beyond the Beyond* (2010). The changes Sterling describes imply ahistoricism more than atemporality, but with the use of atemporality to refer to new forms of cultural practice spreading, it seems that a certain precedent has been set. Moreover, referring to this phenomena as atemporal, allows us to better understand its effects on the temporal experience, which will occupy us later in this essay.

9 "It's 2002—and the decade still has no name," BBC News, http://news.bbc.co.uk/2/hi/uk_ news/1735921.stm. For a collection of mainstream media links on the problem of naming the decade, see http://www.theweek.com/article/index/103534/ Why_cant_we_name_this_decade. Also see http://www.naughtyaughty.com/.

10 Compare with Jameson, *Postmodernism*, 311.

11 A much-expanded version of this essay serves as the first chapter on my book on Network Culture and contains an extended section on modernity and postmodernity. See http://varnelis.net/ network_culture/1_time_history_under_atemporality.

12 Baudrillard. *The Illusion of the End*, 9.

13 Baudrillard "The End of the Millennium or the Countdown," *Economy and Society* 26, no. 4 (1997): 451.

14 http://madmenfootnotes.com/.

15 David Colman, "Dress Codes; The All-American Back from Japan," *New York Times,* June 18, 2009, http://query.nytimes.com/gst/fullpage.html?res=9D00 E1DE153AF93BA25755C0A96F9C8B63.

16 Bruno Latour, "From Realpolitick to Dingpolitick or How to Make Things Public," in Bruno Latour and Peter Weibel, *Making Things Public: Atmospheres of Democracy* (Cambridge, MA: MIT Press, 2005), 30.

17 David Ho, "Tick. Tick. Tick. Will the Cell Phone Slay the Wristwatch?" *Cox News Service* (September 1, 2008), http://www.coxwashington.com/news/content/reporters/stories/2008/30/2008/09/01/ WATCHES01_1STLD_COX.html.

18 Richard Seyler Ling, *The Mobile Connection: The Cell Phone's Impact on Society* (San Francisco: Morgan Kaufmann, 2004), 73.

19 Ling sees this as the most important aspect of mobile telephony, 58.

20 Kenneth J. Gergen, *The Saturated Self: Dilemmas of Identity in Contemporary Life* (New York: Basic Books, 2000).

21 Eric Baumer, Mark Sueyoshi, and Bill Tomlinson, "Exploring the Role of the Reader in the Activity of Blogging," in *Proceeding of the twenty-sixth annual SIGCHI conference on Human factors in computing systems.* Florence, Italy: ACM, 2008, http://doi.acm.org/10.1145/1357054.1357228.

22 Doreen B. Massey, *Space, Place, and Gender* (Minneapolis: University of Minnesota Press, 1994), 119.

23 Mark Fisher, *Capitalist Realism: Is There No Alternative?* (Hampshire, UK: Zero Books, 2009).

24 Luc Boltanski and Eve Chiapello, *The New Spirit of Capitalism* (New York: Verso, 2005).

25 Kazys Varnelis, ed. *Networked Publics* (Cambridge, MA: The MIT Press, 2006), 154. See also Gergen, *The Saturated Self;* and Brian Holmes, "The Flexible Personality: For A New Cultural Critique," http://www.16beavergroup.org/brian/.

26 This idea relies on Jean Baudrillard's concept of the simulation, but in its very language, the simulation still holds out a premise that it is produced by the media industry for us to occupy indirectly. Immediated reality is produced by everyone, constantly, and the media industry's influences fades in it, or rather is transformed.

27 John Tomlinson, *The Culture of Speed: The Coming of Immediacy* (London: Sage, 2007), 74–75, 99. Zygmunt Bauman. *Liquid Modernity* (Cambridge, UK: Polity Press, 2000).

28 Jeffrey Nealon, *Foucault Beyond Foucault: Power and Its Intensifications Since 1984* (Stanford, CA: Stanford University Press, 2008), 63. On the dominance of the economy by finance, see Kevin Phillips, *Bad Money: Reckless Finance, Failed Politics, and the Global Crisis of American Capitalism* (New York: Viking, 2009), xiii. Phillips points out the "extraordinary rise of the U.S. financial sector from 11–12 percent of the gross national product back in the 1980s to a stunning 20–21 percent of the U.S. gross domestic product by 2004–2005. During that same quarter century, manufacturing, for a century the pillar of our economy, slipped from about 25 percent to just 12 percent." The recent economic crisis has not reversed the trend.

29 The article quotes economist Myron Scholes as saying that the analysts took a "view of the world that was far more benign than it was reasonable to take, emphasizing recent inputs over more historic numbers," says Mr. Scholes." See "Efficiency and Beyond," *The Economist,* July 16, 2009, http://www.economist.com/displaystory.cfm?story_id=14030296.

30 Charles Duhigg, "Stock Traders Find Speed Pays, in Milliseconds," *New York Times,* July 23, 2009, http://www.nytimes.com/2009/07/24/business/24trading.html.

31 Gopal Balakrishnan, "Speculations on the Stationary State," *The New Left Review,* no. 59 (2009).

32 Fredric Jameson, *The Political Unconscious: Narrative as a Socially Symbolic Act* (Ithaca, NY: Cornell University Press, 1981), ix.

Robotic Chair (http://www.youtube.com/
watch?v=qR_WjyuRLs4&feature).
Max Dean, Raffaello D'Andrea, and Matt Donovan.
Photo: Nichola Feldman-Kiss.

Hod,
  The field of robotics has begun to relinquish design control to self-assembly and feedback-based mechanisms. The Robotic Chair, *for example, is a robot which collapses itself, relocates its scattered parts, and then reassembles itself, before the cycle starts again. Architects have often designed chairs in a way that embodies the overall design strategy of their work. This robotic chair represents a potential to rethink the discipline in terms of intelligent and thinking architecture. As a designer at the forefront of the robotics movement, what do you believe are the benefits of such a surrender, and how can this research impact the larger scale of the built environment?*
  —Eds.

Hod Lipson

is a roboticist working at the intersection of mechanical engineering, computer science, and biology. His areas of research include evolutionary robotics, design automation, additive manufacturing, and artificial life. He is currently the director of Cornell University's Computational Synthesis Lab (CCSL).

Self-reflective Architecture

One of the most unique and fascinating aspects of intelligent living systems is their ability to self-reflect: to reconstruct "models" of their own morphology and of their own behavior, then use those models to plan how to adapt to new circumstances. Self-reflection plays a key role in accelerating adaptation by reducing costs of physical trial and error and by increasing reliability. While there is a growing trend toward *reactive architecture,* few systems have the second-order ability to reflect. Yet reflective processes, I argue, will soon prove essential in achieving adaptive capacities at all scales—from simple structures to complex cities.

Over the past decades, the cross-fertilization of architectural design and other science and engineering disciplines has led to many new ideas. One of the trends that has been evident in the last decade or so is parametric design. Introduced in the early 90s in mechanical engineering computer-aided-design software, the idea of dimension-driven designs allowed for rapid adaptation of virtual models to ever-changing needs. Parametric modeling has now become mainstream.

One of the more recent trends is the blurring of disciplinary lines between architecture and robotics, a field that involves the study and design of moving machines that react and interact with their environment. In robotics circles, the interaction with architecture has led to the design of new robotic systems that have architecture-scale components and principles, such as self-reconfiguring habitats and tensegrity robots,

Search for Tensegrity, Simon Fivat
Cornell University.

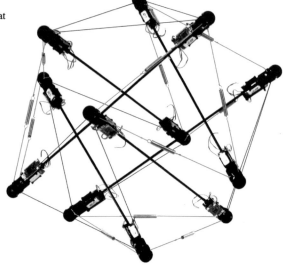

while in architecture, robotic principles have manifested themselves in the form of reactive and responsive systems. More complex behaviors can be achieved, for example, by facades that can respond dynamically to sunlight, wind, noise, and other environmental conditions. The trend of responsive architecture opened the door to systems that react to their environments in interesting new ways. In particular, in adapting to changing conditions, they can potentially meet new goals that are not attainable with static structures whose interplay between function and form needs to be anticipated well in advance, at the design stage. Like parametric design, one of the key merits of reactive and responsive systems is their capacity to adapt. The difference is that parametric design adaptability usually stops when the design process stops. Robotic architecture keeps on adapting.

Hyposurface (http://hyposurface.org).

Beyond Reactive Systems

With the potential benefits of reactive and responsive architecture, however, came the drawbacks that are already well known to any roboticist. The first challenge is the increased reliability issues associated with such systems: more opportunities for failure, and more dramatic consequences. The increased complexity of these dynamic systems makes it more difficult to anticipate the modes of failure in advance and account for them by design. Maintenance of such systems becomes more difficult and costly, and so their longevity comes into question. We settle for responsive systems that will continue to operate for only a few years. Design life-cycle also shortens, with robotic technologies changing on a rapid schedule.

One of the biggest challenges with complex reactive systems such as the responsive walls is that they are difficult to program. These structures are typically modular and composed of many identical units, each sensing and reacting to local stimuli. While the behavior of a single unit can be readily programmed and understood, the behavior of the ensemble of units is difficult to anticipate, let alone program or design. This is especially true when the interaction between modules in the systems involves feedback loops and delays that cause certain phenomena to propagate in nontrivial ways. Even the simplest nonlinear feedback loops can give rise to random-looking chaotic dynamics. These less-apparent "emergent" behaviors are sometimes fascinating, but often frustratingly difficult to control.

The programming problem can be circumvented to some degree using a simulator. As with many robotic systems, once the dynamic response of an individual component can be expressed numerically, then the behavior of an ensemble of units can be simulated in tandem to yield a virtual instantiation of the system. When this dynamic simulation is hooked up to graphic visualization, a designer can then tweak the behavior of an individual module and observe the resulting response of the ensemble. The process can be iterated through trial and error until satisfactory performance is obtained. In fact, if the design goal can be described quantitatively, the tweaking process can be automated. For example, if units in a responsive wall need to be programmed such that they give rise to wave-like reflective patterns, then a simple computer program can be written to start out with a random controller, and repeatedly improve it by testing random variations in the simulator until the desired wave propagation effect is reached. But this approach has its limits too: the limit of simulation fidelity. Many dynamical systems are difficult to simulate because their motion depends critically on minute aspects of the design, such as friction and bifurcations. Just like it is practically impossible to develop a simulator that can accurately predict the resting state of rolling dice, it is practically impossible to accurately predict the behavior of, say, a facade of swinging pendulums, or some other dynamic systems. It is simply too complex to simulate.

Looking at robotics again for inspiration, we can anticipate that the next step involves learning. As the complexity of the dynamics prevents direct prediction, we resort to online learning. Learning systems test various behaviors in reality, and see what works and what does not. Through some mechanism, behaviors that achieve the desired results (or approach it) receive positive reinforcement, and take precedence over behaviors that perform less well. Imagine, for example, a legged robot that needs to learn how to walk. A perfectly predictive simulator of a legged robot is difficult to obtain because of the very same reasons just described: friction is difficult to model yet is critically important, as well as sensor noise and actuator delays. Instead of simulation, the robot can *physically* try out some random motions in reality, and measure its actual forward progress for each of these. It can then take the better ones, try variations of each of those, and so on. After a while, it may end up with a decent locomotion pattern that results in the robot moving forward, without having needed a simulation at all. One can imagine a responsive wall that learns: two big buttons allow patrons to tell the wall whether they like or dislike its behaviors. Through trial and error and incremental improvements, the wall gradually finds out what works and what does not. It can adapt to trends and to changes. A wall installed in Europe might develop an entirely different behavior than the same wall installed in South America, catering to local tastes and cultures.

But physical learning has its limits too. As would be obvious to anyone implementing the learning-wall concept, the learning process is slow, costly, and sometimes risky. The system could wear out by doing too many physical trials, or alienate potential users by exhibiting a series of undesirable behaviors.

Three Generations of Robotics

The hypothetical architectural projects described above resemble a series of real projects performed at the Computational Synthesis Lab since 2001, in an attempt to produce increasingly sophisticated robots. The classic design methodology for most robotics systems is to laboriously design and program them. After several design iterations, a functional robot results. If the design is parametric, then a robot with longer legs, wider chassis, or taller wheels can be generated rapidly and adjusted for new situations. All is well, as long as the tasks for this robot are well defined and anticipated in advance.

But when robots need to deal with unanticipated situations, they need to learn from their experience. Many of the learning systems involve a simulation: the tasks that the robot needs to accomplish can be programmed, tested, and optimized automatically within the simulator. In a test-project in 2000, a simple kinematic simulator was used to automate the design of both the morphology (body) and control (brain) of robots.[1] Starting with a vat of robot components— bars, joints, motors, sensors, and neurons—we allowed a simulated evolutionary process to breed robots for the task of locomotion. After several generations of junk, a few simple machines emerged, which were then perfected over hundreds of simulated generations into a variety of crawling machines. To our excitement, these simple machines worked in reality.

Unfortunately, however, as the robots became more complex, exploiting nonlinear dynamics, friction, and other effects that are difficult to simulate, our simulators began to fail in their predictions. What worked in simulation did not necessarily transfer correctly into reality. We had reached what is known as "the simulation-reality gap."

In desperation, we abandoned the simulation track and had the robots learn directly in physical reality. We constructed a sophisticated pneumatically actuated robot, with enough power to jump around in interesting ways. Through a process of evolution, the robot gradually generated increasingly sophisticated ways to move forward, from random flailing to, finally, coordinated galloping-like locomotion. The process seemed to work, but its drawback was evident: the learning was slow and energetically costly. The robot began to wear out as it learned. We could only sustain this process for a short while. We were stuck in a challenging dichotomy: Learn in simulation, but be limited to the fidelity of the simulator, or learn in reality, but be limited by the costs and risks of physical reality.

Nonaped, Viktor Zykov, Cornell University.

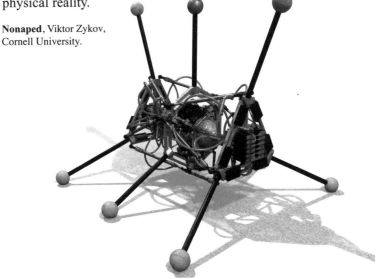

Self-reflective Systems

The solution to the simulation-reality conundrum came through the idea of self-reflection: the robot constructs its own simulator, so that the simulator's fidelity improves together with the performance of the robot. As the robot learns to do new things, the robot's simulator learns how to better simulate those activities. The robot and its simulator develop commensurately, the robot using the simulator to develop new behaviors, and data collected from those behaviors used to improve the simulator. We call that self-reflection because the robot essentially develops a self-image by reexamining its own experience.

We tested this concept on a four-legged robot.[2] The robot has eight motors in total, one at the hip and one at the knee of each leg. It also has two tilt-sensors that report the degree to which the central body is tilting forward-backward and left-right. Using these eight motors and two sensors, the robot needs to learn how to walk. The challenge is, however, that the robot does not *know* that it has four legs. In fact, it does not know its morphology at all. Is it a snake? Is it a spider? It has no clue.

To understand what this means, imagine yourself sitting inside a black box, with no windows. You have access to eight knobs that actuate eight motors but you don't know how the eight motors are connected to the box. As you turn the knobs you can feel how the box is tilting left and right, forward and backward. You now need to find a sequence of knob turns that will make the robot move in a straight line. What can you do? You could, of course, randomly turn the knobs and through a long sequence of trial and error, inch your way forward. But that is slow, energetically costly, and risky: you might accidentally tip over. Instead, you apply self-reflection. This scenario may not be unlike what a brain of a newborn child feels in its new body.

The self-reflective process proceeds as follows: we start with a blank robot simulator—one that hardly predicts anything correctly. Initially, the robot makes a series of random motions (a). As it undergoes these motions, it records the tilt angles sensed for each of the motor positions. Using the resulting set of observed motor commands and the corresponding angles, it tries to come up with several hypotheses of what it might look like. Some hypotheses about its own shape may explain the data better than others. Since there is only little data at this point, there are many valid hypotheses that are different from each other yet are each consistent with the observations. The robot arrives at a series of valid self-image hypotheses (b). Although when we look at them we can see that most of them are wrong, insofar as the robot knows, they are all valid. The robot then tries to figure out what motor command to perform next to *rule out* some of these hypotheses. It chooses a set of motor commands that would elicit the most *disagreement* in the predictions of competing hypotheses. Just like a scientist designs an experiment that causes the most disagreement between predictions of competing theories in order to eliminate one theory, so will the results from this robot action eliminate some of the wrong self-models. The robot then physically performs that action (a), and records the angles. This new data is then used to eliminate some models and improve others, and the cycle (a)–(c) repeats until only one self-model remains, or the set of self-models cannot be made to disagree in their predictions, implying they are essentially equivalent. The robot then uses that self-model to plan how to walk (d). Because the self-model is fairly accurate, what makes the self-model move also makes the physical robot move (e). The bottom line is that the robot has learned how to move after making only a few physical motions, and self-reflecting quite a bit.

To test this idea further, we removed one of the legs of the robot to mimic damage. The robot started walking, but the tilt angles predicted by the intact model did not correspond to the actual tilt angles sensed, suggesting that the self-model was no longer correct. The robot went back into the (a)–(c) cycle, making a series of moves until the newly generated model reflected its missing leg. The resulting new motion plan was a limping-type locomotion pattern, and indeed the robot began to limp. Perhaps not the most elegant locomotion, but it worked: the robot did not have a sensor and program that said "leg came off, switch to motion plan B." Instead, it adapted spontaneously.

Self-reflective Structures

As architecture and infrastructure become increasingly complex, they too require more adaptive capabilities. They need to recover from damage, adapt to new usage patterns, and accommodate design changes. Consider, for example, a simple self-reflecting truss bridge. Traditionally, a truss bridge would need to be inspected on a regular basis to ensure its integrity. Imagine, however, that the bridge had the ability to self-reflect. The bridge would be able to actuate itself in various ways, for example, by applying subtle vibrations at various points and various frequencies, using preinstalled buzzers. At other locations on the bridge, it could sense and record these vibrations. The bridge would initially induce some random vibrations and sense the responses at the sensors, and from this relationship of actuation and sensation it could create models of itself. This set of self-models might contain various competing candidate hypotheses about what the bridge actually looks like, but only one of them will be correct. The bridge will then seek out which actuators and what frequencies to vibrate itself, again in a way that causes these models to disagree in their predictions. It will then perform that action, and use the sensations to rule out some models and improve others. The final self-model would be a realistic, data-driven model of the bridge. If the bridge had some weak link, so would the model. In this way, the self-model can be used to detect damage, to identify a weakening joint, or to pinpoint a region that is under more stress than anticipated. Such self-reflecting infrastructure could lead to more adaptive and self-monitoring systems.

To test this idea, we applied it to a virtual bridge, subjecting a small amount of damage to one of its members. We showed that the bridge could detect that fault faster and more accurately than conventional civil-engineering methods.[3]

Increasingly, new buildings use some sort of computer model to determine the optimal design. It is not unusual to use a structural-thermal numerical simulation of a building to predict the effects of internal air flow, wind, solar incidence, and other weather effects, and to use those predictions to optimize the design of windows, HVAC systems, and other aspects. Many buildings will even have a central controller that will use various sensors to adapt various aspects, such as heating, cooling, and air circulation, to new situations. These systems are reminiscent of the days of early robotics, when the robot was simulated perfectly, and its behavior programmed based on this simulation.

Self-simulating Buildings

But if the field of robotics is to serve as a guide, then this trend will not scale. Computer simulations of buildings will ultimately not be predictive *enough*. They will not be able to accommodate the chaotic nature of some aspects, or identify which aspects need to be modeled and which can be ignored. Even if the model is perfect at the time of construction, it will soon become out of date as design changes are introduced, new unanticipated usage patterns emerge, or the environment changes: perhaps a new building is built outdoors casting a shadow on a previously sunny side, or changing the local wind patterns. Sooner rather than later, the model will be inadequate. Like robotics, it is best if the building maintains its own simulator. The building actuates and senses, and based on this information updates it own simulator—its own *self-image*. It then uses that simulator to plan. If predictions fail, the new information can be used to further adapt the simulator, and so on.

It is not always obvious what a system should model and how the self-model should be represented internally. A building could model how temperature and energy flow within and around it, depending on usage patterns and weather conditions, and use those predictions to react to future changes. This self-model, however, will not necessarily look like a traditional architectural model, with well-defined geometric primitives and attributes. Like the self-image of a human, this self-model will likely be more like a neural-network of influences and relationships whose dynamic behavior predicts reality, but whose form has nothing to do with it. A building with moving walls could reflect and create models of people's interaction with objects, and use those models to blend better with its surroundings. A traffic network would not have models of vehicles and roads; it would create models of driver behaviors, from impatient commuters to bewildered tourists, and use the collective behavior of many such models to determine optimal traffic-light schedules.

At the scale of a building, the reactive project has been initiated crudely by such realized projects as Edison's *Black Maria* or Koolhaas's *Transformer*, which respond to changes in solar orientation or program (respectively) by changing their direction.

PradaTransformer, Coutresy of AMO*OMA.

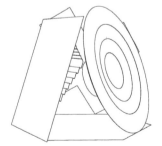  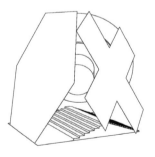 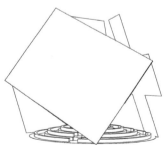

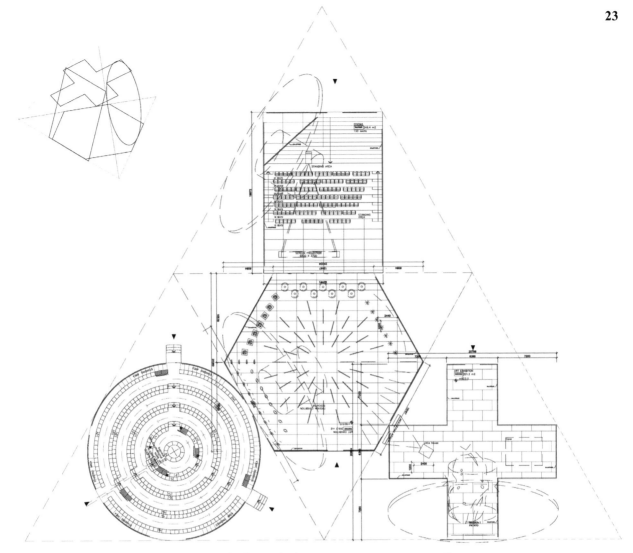

These systems, in the future, could not only forgo the horses or cranes necessary for their dynamism, but the building could think for itself. There is no reason to stop at architecture—this concept can be applied to any scale of construction. In the future, every critical urban element—from a responsive wall to a complex transportation network—could be self-reflecting. These systems would continuously create and update their own self-models, and use these self-models to detect malfunction or to optimize and plan ahead. *That* is something to reflect on …

Endnotes

1 H. Lipson and J.B. Pollack, "Automatic Design and Manufacture of Robotic Lifeforms," *Nature 406* (2000): 974–978.

2 J. Bongard, V. Zykov, and H. Lipson "Resilient Machines Through Continuous Self-Modeling," *Science*, vol. 314, no. 5802(2006): 1118–1121.

3 W. Aquino, B. Kouchmeshky, J. Bongard, and H. Lipson "Co-Evolutionary Algorithm for Structural Damage Identification Using Minimal Physical Testing," *International Journal for Numerical Methods in Engineering.*

4 M. Schmidt and H. Lipson "Distilling Free-Form Natural Laws from Experimental Data," *Science*, vol. 324, no. 5923 (2009): 81–85.

Feedback Man, Lydia Kallipoliti, *Log* 13/14,
Fall 2008, 115–118.

Lydia Kallipoliti

Feedback Man

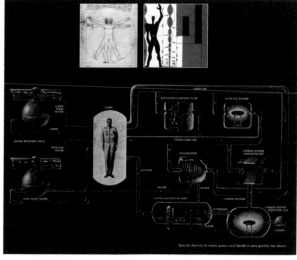

NASA Langley Research Center, 1960. Four men are enclosed and monitored for four months in a living simulator, a hermetically sealed environment called the NASA living pod. In order to survive without additional provisions inside this experimental spaceship, in order for man to venture into outer space, where the environmental conditions are inhospitable to his physiology (as NASA tells us),[1] it is necessary that all human waste be converted to oxygen, water, and, hopefully, food. The General Dynamics diagram for a life-support system[2] visualizes the problem of monitoring, capturing, and recycling human subsystems. As we can witness, a new biotechnological image of man emerges, one in which human agency is delegated in terms of input and output.[3] At the same time, the diagram shows man entirely bound to his environment, since only with the service of digesters, converters, dryers, and dehumidifiers can all cycles of ingestion and excretion be closed and redirected back into the body.

The General Dynamics diagram was reproduced in several architectural publications,[4] including *Architectural Design*, *Bau*[5] and *Adhocism*, portraying the new vision of man and the space he inhabits (shrinking the natural world) as if he were tied to its walls and parts with an umbilical cord. In many respects, architectural drawings of man are a measure of worlds, an image personifying the architecture of different eras. Thus, Vitruvian Man, inscribed in a circle, speaks of a period of geometrical supremacy (Renaissance humanism), while Le Corbusier's Modulor, measured on an external reference line, is an architectonic vision of idealized proportions underwriting modern architecture.[6] Now, however, the General Dynamics diagram projects the materiality of the body dissolved in a series of flows and feedback loops compressed into a space suit or a pod.

The image of man as a heroic explorer who overcomes his given physiological boundaries and conquers uninhabitable lands was of larger cultural interest in the 1960s, projecting the astronaut as a new universal human subject. "Astronauts are envoys of mankind," states the Outer Space Treaty of the United Nations in 1966.[7] The astronaut, masked and geared, became a positive figure of unbounded progress, equipped to carry in his space suit and functional vesture a

GENERAL DYNAMICS LIFE SUPPORT SYSTEM. TOP LEFT: THE VITRUVIAN MAN, BY LEONARDO DA VINCI. TOP RIGHT: LE CORBUSIER'S MODULOR. IMAGE COURTESY THE AUTHOR.

piece of the Earth's environment. Outer space, the bottom of oceans, Antarctica – exceptionally unfriendly regions to the physiology of humans – were all part of an envisioned new democratic political reality. Outer space and its corollary regions were places for all that defied property and territorial commitment. In this vast, blank space, humanity had a second chance to reinvent itself from scratch.

This "democratic" venture came at a very high, almost deadly cost, however, with the resurgence of a primitive fear that a man could be buried in the combustive products of his own body. In case of a systemic malfunction, excrement could kill him or contaminate his environmental "egosphere."[8] In this sense, the system could not be anything less than 100-percent foolproof, with compulsory regeneration its maxim and material loss negligible or nonexistent within the closed state. Inhabited space was in the faithful service of closing all loops: a capsule furnished with units embedded in the walls to collect urine, carbon dioxide, and floating human waste – all necessary parts in order to accumulate waste and facilitate feedback.

1. The sealing of four men in the NASA Langley Simulator is narrated in NASA's promotional motion picture for television, *The Case for Regeneration* (1960). Motion Picture No. 255-HQ-131A, Special Media Archives Services Division, National Archives, College Park, MD.
2. The NASA Langley Simulator was a collaborative project between General Dynamics and the NASA Langley Research Center.
3. See Peder Anker, "The Ecological Colonization of Space," *Environmental History* 10, no. 2 (2005): 239–68. See also Peder Anker, "The Closed World of Ecological Architecture," *The Journal of Architecture* 10, no. 5 (2005): 527–52.
4. The diagram was first published in the *International Science and Technology* journal in 1966. See "Keeping Alive in Space: A Report from General Dynamics," *International Science and Technology* (February 1966): 52–51.
5. NASA's educational brief, similar to the General Dynamics diagram, was published in *Bau* as well as in *Architectural Design*. The brief concerned the functionality of space suits (specifically oxygen supply) and the elimination of carbon dioxide and moisture.
6. This comment emerged in conversation with Alexandros Tsamis at MIT, March 2008.
7. See the Outer Space Treaty, signed in Geneva in 1966. United Nations Archives, New York, NY.

8. The term *egosphere* is found in Peter Sloterdijk, "Cell Block, Egospheres, Self-Container," *Log* 10 (Summer/Fall 2007).

Dear Lydia,
    In Log *13/14 "Feedback Man," you described the recirculatory systems in NASA's 1960 Living Pod, and the effect of this and similar programs on architecture, stating that while the "Vitruvian Man and the Modular indicate a passage from the cosmos to modernist abstract space ... Feedback Man speaks of an insular, closed, techno-world that requires more information than form and geometry to be envisioned." These relationships address feedback systems in the space of outer space, yet some of the side effects of the space program led to studies of earth-bound feedback systems, which themselves affected the course of architecture.*
    We invite you to elaborate on these earth-bound space programs and their architectural consequences.
    —Eds.

1976:

Architectural Design (AD) magazine publishes an issue on *Autonomous Houses*. At the bottom corner of the cover, a label warns readers: "Autonomous Property. KEEP OUT." By this time, the theme appears logical, if not trite. Following the oil crisis and a decade of dense environmental debates, the terms *self-sufficiency, self-reliance, life-support,* and *living autonomy* are part of a pervasive lexicon for alternative technologies, described by *AD* as an "architectural prevailing cult project" that has preoccupied the British avant-garde scene for a decade. (Cliff Harper, *Autonomous Houses*, *Architectural Design*, July 1972, Wiley-Blackwell/UK.)

1960:

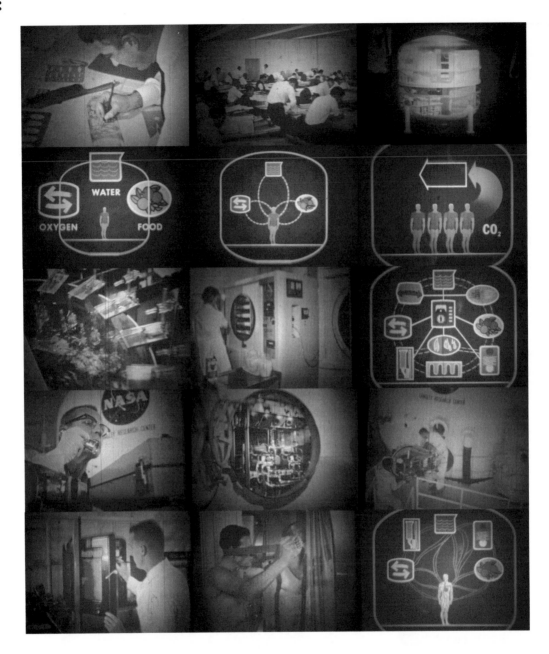

NASA creates a promotional educational motion picture for television titled *Living in Space: The Case for Regeneration.* At this moment, outer space is the ultimate frontier in the context of the space race and the tension of the cold war. They key, however, to the colonization of this territory can no longer be found in the invention of rockets, but within the management and reinvention of human physiology. To transport man into outer space, he would require an artificial environmental Earth bubble. *Recycling, rebreathing, restoration,* and other words indicating the regeneration of human output into viable input, are essential mechanisms that warranty the travel of the living organism into nonliving conditions. (Stills from "Living in Space: The Case for Regeneration," motion picture no. 255-HQ-131A, National Archives. Courtesy of NASA.)

1971:

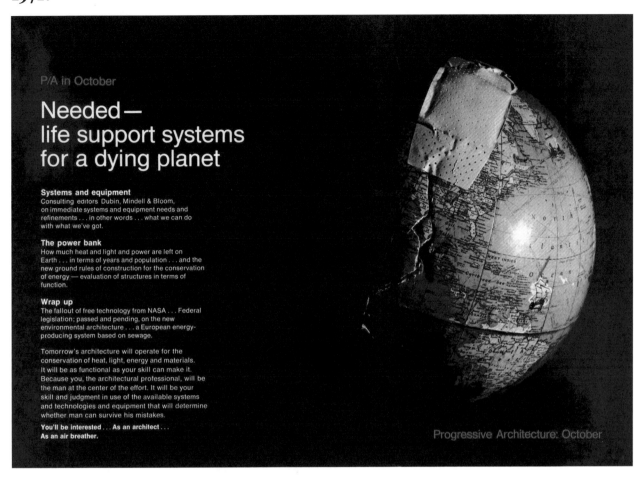

P/A in October

Needed — life support systems for a dying planet

Systems and equipment
Consulting editors Dubin, Mindell & Bloom, on immediate systems and equipment needs and refinements . . . in other words . . . what we can do with what we've got.

The power bank
How much heat and light and power are left on Earth . . . in terms of years and population . . . and the new ground rules of construction for the conservation of energy — evaluation of structures in terms of function.

Wrap up
The fallout of free technology from NASA . . . Federal legislation; passed and pending, on the new environmental architecture . . . a European energy-producing system based on sewage.

Tomorrow's architecture will operate for the conservation of heat, light, energy and materials. It will be as functional as your skill can make it. Because you, the architectural professional, will be the man at the center of the effort. It will be your skill and judgment in use of the available systems and technologies and equipment that will determine whether man can survive his mistakes.

You'll be interested . . . As an architect . . . As an air breather.

Progressive Architecture: October

Progressive Architecture advertises its forthcoming issue in October, with a wounded Earth that calls for help from "architects and air breathers": *Needed—Life Support Systems for a Dying Planet.* The issue suggests learning from the research of the space industry and presents a series of housing schemes as life support systems. Materials and devices used in spaceships are recommended for direct transference to domestic contexts promising high levels of energy renewal. At this moment, the byproduct devices of the space program are promoted in the building industry as salvation mechanisms; they are to battle the blatant environmental crisis of a closed planet that has just been revealed to the eyes of the world as a single image. (Courtesy of Architect/Hanley Wood.)

1972:

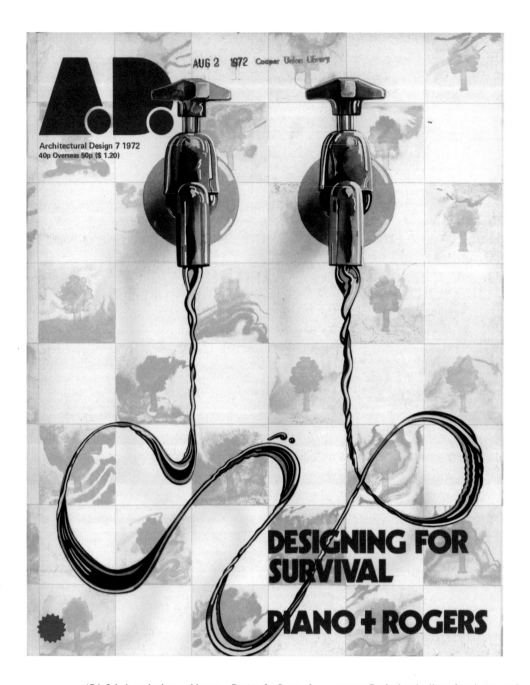

AD's July issue invites architects to *Design for Survival.* The cover features a water flow that detours from one tap to another and suggests that household effluent streams recirculate endlessly. This water feedback showcases an unprecedented fascination with the ecological household as a self-sufficient, autonomous, and regenerative unit, capable of harnessing its waste and providing its own energy. Backed up by lists of environmental statistics, the issue urges readers to consider that we no longer have a choice about the way we live and the space we live in. Rather, it is a question of survival. At this moment, the household is understood as a synecdoche for the earth as a whole. (Adrian George, *Designing for Survival*, Architectural Design, January 1976, Wiley-Blackwell/UK.)

Lydia Kallipoliti

*is an architect and a writer. She holds architecture degrees from
AUTh in Greece, MIT and Princeton University. Currently, she is
an assistant professor adjunct at the Cooper Union in New York.
Kallipoliti is the editor of "EcoRedux: Design Remedies for a Dying
Planet," a special issue of* Architectural Design (AD) *magazine.
Her design and theoretical work has been published and exhibited
internationally.*

Return to Earth

Feedback Houses

In the four preceding snapshots, we see how the concept of *total circular resource regeneration* migrates from one context to the other: from military research and the experiments of NASA's space program, to the housing industry, to a counter-cultural practice for autonomous living in the city, and finally to the nostalgia of the homesteading movement and the perception of housing communities as self-reliant ecosystems. What remains constant, however, is the emergence of a new environmental consensus in the form of a synthetic naturalism, where the laws of nature and metabolism are displaced from the domain of the wilderness to the domain of cities and buildings. Previous concepts of nature's immaculate preservation and conservation separate from the urban milieu gave rise to a novel naturalism of "artificial ecology," where the functions of operations in nature were copied as precise analogies in man-made systems. Distinctly different from the first environmental era, which rallied for the fresh spirit of the wilderness and the preservation of unindustrialized lands, the rise of modern environmentalism in the 1960s and 1970s called for the replication of natural ecosystems anew in synthetic environments.

The design of a house as a synthetic ecology suggested that a dwelling could reproduce a natural ecosystem; a system of mechanized interrelated parts as a model of a piece of nature. As John McHale argued that the "closed system" ecology of the space capsule was a micro-miniaturized version of our planetary vehicle,[1] the house was meant to embody a microcosm of the earth as a whole. This shift was very much related to the ecologist's appropriation of a scientific language and a set of tools used by cyberneticians in the postwar period.[2] By diagramming the flow of energy in the natural world as input and output, circuits in a feedback loop, cyberneticians provided ecologists with new research techniques and a new biologically informed (but also computational) theory of inhabiting the world. At the same time, the space program played a fundamental role in this reformation of the building industry, effectively adopting, rationalizing, and simulating nature's operations. The smart organization of material flows in spaceships was an issue of survival; life was dependent on the cycling of provisions. The potential for convergence of all waste into useful materials became eminently important as a means of sustaining life within the enclosed space of the spacecraft. In essence, the projection of humanity in outer space was less about the conquering of a new physical and technological frontier and more about the reflection of primordial habitation principles on Earth, as well as the conception of a new type of a recirculatory house, a cybernetic laboratory.

Closed recirculatory systems illustrate, beyond just a cultural fascination with the space program, emerging architectural concerns related to habitation: first, a new integrated structure where the human physiology of ingestion and excretion becomes a combustion device, part of the system that is inhabited. Second, closed recirculatory systems, as organizational divisions of closed loop cycles, are recursive models that generate complex behaviors. Closed recirculatory systems demonstrate an ontological problem of creating an autonomous personal space or a protective environmental enclosure around the human. This spatial paradigm, similar to the bubble space of the astronaut's suit, can be described as an "ego-sphere"[3] that, according to the German philosopher Peter Sloterdjik, alludes to a novel territorial paradigm of the 20th century: modern individualism. Humans may claim their own space around the immediate proximity of their physical bodies and become their own planets.

"Down to Earth": Grumman Integrated Household

In the late 1960s, as the image of the whole earth and the effects of the space program impacted cultural imagination, it was suggested that spacecraft hardware could be directly employed in the building industry, yielding ecological benefits and rendering the house a "life-support system." The house was promoted as a performative machine, capable of providing its own energy and food. This relocation of services resulted in an unprecedented systematization of the household, but more prominently this directive was delivered as NASA's gift to the optimization of architectural design. As one can witness in the "EcoTech" section of *AD,* NASA's integrated utility systems allegedly granted to the building sector the scientific credibility that it so unfavorably lacked: "NASA's contribution to the solution of national problem of natural resources and pollution abatement as related to housing is included in a design of a 500 apartment complex to be built in Houston, Texas."[4]

At the time, Grumman Corporation was a leading firm associated with space research, primarily specializing in bioastronautics, human performance, life-support systems and the habitability of future space stations. Grumman was highly invested in the development of technologies that would make the dream of the space station a reality. However, they were equally interested in "projecting" their inventions for outer space down to earth. This was evidenced by a string of advertisements between 1964 and 1967, in which the company announced that their "plans for outer space are down to earth." Certain experiments in spacecraft life-support systems had not been successful in zero-gravity conditions, mainly due to difficulties of directing bacteria and microzoa flow for anaerobic digestion in waste consumption. However, there were not the same difficulties when used for terrestrial applications.

The corporation consulted with several architectural firms in the late 1960s to design a modular housing unit, a waste disposal system, a sewage system (as in the astronaut's lavatory), and an energy efficiency system for homes that incorporated solar cells for the civil consumer market. These applications, transferred from technologies used in life-support systems for spacecrafts, sold a considerable number of units in the United States under the label Grumman's Integrated Household System. Moreover, Grumman's way of connecting different apparatuses into an integrated building circuit was promoted as an ecological remedy to environmental problems.[5] In 1969, Grumman offered their research program on domestic space and life-support systems to the Department of Housing and Urban Development, an organization charged with the development of improved housing system concepts for large-volume production and the construction of 1,400,000 new dwellings.[6] Yet, offsetting NASA's specific techniques to the building industry resulted in a new kind of fixation with biological substances and physiological flows in the design of the household.

Using NASA's conversion diagrams for spaceships as a starting point, every solid and liquid waste stream was segmented and decomposed to its utter constituents in a tenuous plan to produce drinkable water from collected droplets and oxygen from carbon dioxide. All human waste was to be chemically treated and dissolved into base data that could potentially be reconstructed in new combinations. This approach, labeled as "atomic recycling," operated on the same premises of noiseless conversions that garbage housing projects did. However, atomic recycling carried this initial hypothesis further, through endless segmentations of matter, going down many scales, in the hope of refiguring substance at an atomic level or at the very least that all solid waste could be decomposed to a powderlike material state.

Such "wish-fulfillments" are fundamental to recycling diagrams, if we may borrow Freud's terminology. Even in NASA's most pragmatic graphs for the operations of spaceships, desire plays a key role in the completion of the diagram, by filling in the blanks and legitimizing fuzzy conversions. To understand this claim, we may take as an example the *General Dynamics Life Support System,* an iconic graph for the regeneration of water and air in a space capsule, which carries out a three-step mission: to segment all human input and output in constituent component parts; to map relationships between parts and visually extrapolate a reciprocal organization; and finally, to redirect all human output back into human input. What the diagram fails to explain adequately is the nature of the material conversions that are necessary to chemically resynthesize materials from one state to another. One has to keep in mind that the proposed conversions do not merely involve phase changes, such as solid to liquid to gas, but also impossible responsibilities, such as turning feces into food, and this is precisely where wish fulfillment comes in. Operating under the assumption that a coherent, systemic, organization can be implemented to any material system, the two recycling diagrams contain several "black holes"—fuzzy conversions that could only be accomplished miraculously. In the iconic graph, these "black holes" are visualized as conversion "bubble-like" machines that contain stools and complicated interior mechanisms. They are extra devices added to the system, designed to mediate flows and assume the responsibility to transmute substances, using any technique possible, such as drying, rotating, dehumidifying, electrifying, filtering, oxidizing, and so on.

Under the pseudonym Ruppert Spade, Martin Pawley, in his 1970 article, "Trick Recyclist,"[7] wrote about the unelaborated nature of closed systems' recycling and self-sufficiency. Pawley described the experiments of Mr. Edward Burton, who, between 1960 and 1966, had taken out several patents relating to a Biological Waste Treatments System, with a view to adapting his waste recycling system for use undersea or in space.[8] To develop his inventions, Burton was in touch with the Grumann Corporation in the early 1960s, and translated the

Advertisement of Grumman Corporation in the
International Science and Technology journal.

Grumman's plan

r outer space

are down
to earth

We feel at home in space. So much so, that we've spent $20 million on space facilities, a pretty down-to-earth amount. And we have 3,000 engineers working on space programs. Besides, we have plans.

They're big. But they're also realistic. Even now, Grumman is adapting the LEM vehicle to the following missions:

- Earth orbiting space station for a variety of experiments
- Lunar orbiting space station for gathering scientific data
- Lunar taxi to support extended stays on the moon
- Lunar shelter for astronauts
- Cargo vehicle for a variety of payloads.

And we're not done yet.

These programs are tied in with our nation's post-Apollo objectives. That's part of being down to earth, too.

GRUMMAN *Aircraft Engineering Corporation • Bethpage, L.I., New York*

industry's smart technologies into home-made reprocessing systems, managing the dubious accomplishment of adequately nourishing a duck, 15 goldfish, an apple tree sapling, an apricot tree plantlet, and a small rhododendron plant, singularly from household effluent.[9] With a number of tricky conversions and crafty oxidizing and permeation devices, Burton's system eventually became commercially available in the United States in the early 1970s, promising to grow tomatoes from household effluent.

What we are less aware of is what happened in due course to Burton's flora and fauna after running his Biological Waste Treatments System for extensive periods of time. Recycling systems, especially the aspiring noiseless ones, are absolutely closed systems that redirect all input into output; and as such they are more than likely to exhibit unpredictable behaviors, including the production of new substances that are not calculated to be dealt with by the internal organization of the system. Closed autopoietic systems derail from an original systematized scheme that is designed to run invariant perpetually. Instead, prolific new subsystems feed the original system with new input, constantly changing its internal organization. Pawley's stark criticism on the feasibility of regenerative systems is in resonance with his own frustration on "garbage housing,"[10] which conceptually fulfils a circular system on a planetary scale, feeding the industrial by-products back into the cycle of production as new building materials. It seems that the architect's desire to close the circle is eminent. However, noiseless recycling is an impossible enterprise in time, or an "ecotopia"; and if portrayed as a realistic task, it undoubtedly needed to combine high-tech devices with some "wishful thinking."

From Shit to Food: Graham Caine's Eco-House

One of the earliest ecological houses, the Eco-House, was built in Eltham, South London in 1972, as a laboratory and living experiment by Graham Caine, a member of the anarchist group Street Farmers, originally formed by Peter Crump and Bruce Haggart. The Eco-House was a fully functional integrated system that converted human waste to methane for cooking, as well as maintained a hydroponic greenhouse with radishes, tomatoes, and even bananas. Caine, then a 26-year-old fourth-year student at the Architectural Association of London, designed and built the Eco-House as an "inhabitable housing laboratory" that would grow vegetables out of household effluents and fertilize the land with reprocessed organic waste. With a £2,000 fund from Alvin Boyarski, the chairman of the AA, and scavenged materials, Caine settled in the house in December 1972. After having lived in the house for two years with his family, Caine was asked to destroy it in 1975. By that time, the Eco-House had received wide attention from the British press and architectural magazines, as well as considerable attention in television. It was the main subject of a television show titled *Clearings of a Concrete Jungle* in BBC's Open Programme for Television in June 1973. The broadcast was featured in the London *Radio Times* with the promotional line: "Spring is here and the time is ripe for planting in the streets." Other titles in the British press included: "The House that Grows" and "A New Way of Living" in the London *Garden News,* "Living off the Sun in South London" in *The Observer,* and "A Revolutionary Structure" in *Oz* magazine.[11]

Eco House in *AD*. Courtesy of Grahame Caine.

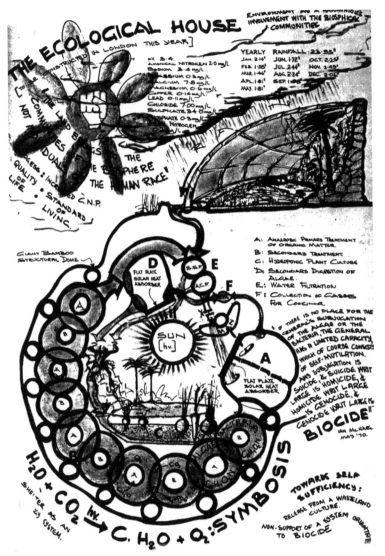

Throughout the process, Caine used himself and his family as guinea pigs in order to test the function of several components of the house. He experimented with his waste, his cooking habits, his use of water, monitoring closely every activity of daily practice until the day the house was demolished in 1974. Caine was undoubtedly the steward of the house; he alone knew how to feed the house with the right nutrients—how to chop wood, grow plants, irrigate the greenhouse, and supply the engines. The architect, therefore, was an indispensable biological part of the house, connected to it in a diagram where excretion becomes a vital constituent of the system's sustenance. In many respects, the house was more grown than constructed. It needed attention from its caretaker, and without human presence its living biotechnical systems would degenerate and die. Describing his house as a life-support system, Caine satirically commented that the architect may now relate to his own shit.[12]

In the unpublished addendum to the periodical *Street Farmer* 2, the Eco-House is referenced as a "spaceship" on earth. However, self-sufficiency was understood by Caine and the Street Farmers, as a political statement against consumerism and capitalism. The Eco-House embodied for its builders a grain of resistance against the state's networks of centralized control. According to Caine, capitalism could be illustrated in a linear scheme, while the recycling of organic matter, the collection of rainwater and sunshine that in its turn produces food, gas, and heating, represents an alternative political reality of cyclical behaviors where material can be used and reused perpetually.[13]

In many ways, this detachment from the main urban supply networks depicts a collective repudiation for the urban condition, which is portrayed by both the counter-culture and the space program as a catastrophic environment that restrains the imagination and the freedom of the individual. In this sense, the Eco-House becomes an island, uprooted from its urban context, like its own planet, but very much in exchange with physiological parameters: temperature, water, light, humidity, and so forth calculated in numeric data. We may perceive this detachment, outlined as an ecological and political imperative, as a fundamental reorientation of the house in relationship to its urban condition.

Weaving Caine's political assertions to the premises of NASA's by-products for the building indsutry, it is striking to observe how the same cybernetic prescription of a system migrates from the military complex to a countercultural political theory. On the one hand, NASA's scenario for self-sufficiency comprises a project of technological supremacy and regards mostly the invention of hardware in order to conquer a new frontier, now visible and detectable to our eyes; the colonial modality is evident in this aspiration to master the new land, or space, even if out of oxygen. On the other hand, the equipped interior of the Eco-House is portrayed as the fantasy of an "exterior" to the political reality. The interior, armed with digesters, becomes a strategy of political autonomy to withdraw from the tentacles of society and the state's organizational infrastructure, away from the authoritative networks to which people must yield. The Grumman Integrated Household and the Eco-House, despite representing two very different political realities and existential problems, come to be expressed by the same strategy for self-reliance.

Despite all odds, the ongoing experiment of the enclosed space was ceremoniously revived in the massive Biosphere 2 project in Arizona, which was completed and sealed in 1991. Not surprisingly, fresh air had to be injected and food introduced to ensure the health of the sealed subjects. But even beyond ecological tourist attractions, the spaceship lives on in the thousands of sick buildings of corporate America. Sealed, heavily air-conditioned buildings usually generate problematic airborne conditions, resulting from a building's lack of exchange with its surrounding environment. In most sick buildings, there cannot be an identifiable cause for illness, as a causal effect of a specific deficiency. A 1984 World Health Organization Committee report suggested that up to 30 percent of new and remodeled buildings worldwide may be the subject of excessive complaints related to indoor air quality and suffer from what is known as the *sick building syndrome,* a term describing situations in which building occupants experience acute health and comfort effects linked to the time spent in a building.

Recycling waste, either organic or inorganic, was fundamental to the rising discourse of ecological design. The real question submitted with this study is how biological and environmental processes invade the domestic realm and the practice of everyday life; how the division and distribution of organic, growing matter is vital for the sustenance of the house's health. It is finally critical to observe that in the rise of postwar ecological design theories, recycling was more than a technical task; it was a psychosocial position for the migration of life via the phase change of material substances. From this viewpoint, matter does not come to an end, it is not wasted; instead it changes its state. Recycling, therefore, is not just about the formation of new materials, but also about the transference and migration of properties from one substance to another, and all of the intermediate stages of a productive cycle.

In a recent NASA conference in Washington, DC, in October 2007, a common consensus surfaced in honor of the 50 years celebration of outer space research. Officers and researchers claimed that the space program's greater accomplishments were not what they were intended to be; not the conquering of the new frontier, and the actual moon-landing; but the space program's side effects: such were the photographs of the Earth. Likewise, this successful derailment, an incidental by-product shaped as a discipline undergoes a transformation, may suggest an alternative reading of architectural history, not by offering actual objects and a new paradigm, but by suggesting new tools and new modes of practice. The objects may be fictional, impossible, or in the best-case scenario, ephemeral, but architecture is mostly a project of the imagination. The objects can be ephemeral, but the tools and modalities of design creativity that they produce are not.

Endnotes

1 John McHale, "Outer Space," in *Architectural Design,* vol. 37 (February 1967): 67. See also John McHale, *The Future of the Future* (New York: George Brazilier, 1969).

2 See Peder Anker, "The Ecological Colonization of Space," *Environmental History* 10, no. 2 (2005): 239–268. See also Peder Anker, "The Closed World of Ecological Architecture," *The Journal of Architecture* 10, no. 5 (2005): 527–552.

3 The term *egosphere* was coined by Peter Sloterdijk in his article "Cell Block, Egospheres, Self-Container," in *Log* 10 (Summer/Fall 2007).

4 "NASA integrated utility system," in the "Eco-Tech" section *of Architectural Design*, vol. 43 (February 1973): 74.

5 See Anker, "The Closed World of Ecological Architecture," 539.

6 See Ruppert Spade, "Trick Recyclist" in the "Cosmorama" section of *Architectural Design*, vol. 40 (March 1970): 111–112.

7 Spade, "Trick Recyclist," 112.

8 Ibid.

9 Ibid.

10 See Martin Pawley, "Garbage Housing," in *Architectural Design,* vol. 41, no. 2 (1971): 86–95; Martin Pawley, "Chile and the Cornell Programme," in *Architectural Design*, vol. 43, no. 12 (1973): 777–784; Martin Pawley, "Garbage Housing," in *Architectural Design*, vol. 43, no. 12 (1973): 647–776. See also Martin Pawley, *Garbage Housing* (London, UK: Architectural Press, 1975).

11 The Eco-House was published in the following publications: Glenn Barker, "A New Way of Living," in *Garden News,* no. 780 (June 15, 1973); Grahame Caine, "A Revolutionary Structure," in *Oz* (November 1972): 12–13. Supplemented by Mike Moore's diagrams based on Grahame Caine's originals; Gerald Leach (Science Correspondent), "Living off the Sun in South London," in *The Observer* (August 27, 1972); Grahame Caine, "The Eco-House," in Bruce Haggart, Peter Crump (eds.), *Street Farmer,* no. 1 & no. 2 (London, 1971–1972); Grahame Caine, "The Ecological House," in *Architectural Design* (March 1972): 140–141; Grahame Caine, "Street Farmhouse," in Stefan Szcelkun (ed.), *Survival Scrapbook, vol. 5: Energy* (Bristol, UK: Unicorn Bookshop Press, 1975); Grahame Caine, "The Eco-House," in *Mother Earth News* (March/April 1973); Grahame Caine, Bruce Haggart, and Peter Crump, "Some Proposals on the Reservicing of an Urban Terraced House," in John Prenis (ed.), *Domeletter,* no. 4 (Philadelphia, PA: Self-published, 1972). See the archives of the Architectural Association, London; Eve Williams, "The House that Grows" (based on an interview with Grahame Caine), in *Garden News,* no. 722 (London, May 5, 1972): 13; Glen Barker, "A New Way of Living," in *Garden News,* no. 780 (London, June 15, 1973): 3.

12 Grahame Caine, "A Revolutionary Structure," in *Oz* (November 1972): 12–13. Supplemented by Mike Moore's diagrams based on Grahame Caine's originals.

13 Author's personal interview with Graham Caine in Ronda, Spain (January 8th, 2008).

Dear Jason and Aleksandr,

The United States produces approximately 250 million tons of garbage each year, of which 83 million tons is recycled or composted, equivalent to a 33.2 percent recycling rate, a figure that has been rising since the 1960s.[1] But there is another kind of waste produced that is much harder to quantify and to recycle. Physical manifestations of this less tangible refuse can be found locally in the cities of the Rust Belt and among the networks of canals throughout New York State. Embedded within these fossils, there exist whole bodies of knowledge connected to those superseded modes of production and obsolete infrastructures. As technology and interests shift, and we realize that certain systems are outdated, irrelevant, and insufficient: that knowledge is at risk of being lost.

Can you describe how we might recycle, in addition to our trash, some of this intellectual waste, and what the consequences of this might be on the physical realm?

—Eds.

Austin + Mergold

is an architecture, landscape, and design practice based in Philadelphia. A+M is engaged in a wide range of work with a special interest for re-interpretation of the local vernacular. Jason Austin is also an adjunct professor at University of Pennsylvania, Department of Landscape Architecture and Temple University, Department of Architecture. Aleksandr Mergold is a visiting assistant professor at Cornell University Department of Architecture.

Yes We Can

Some Musings on Canning and Infrastructural Metamorphoses

Cannery Row is a poem, a stink, a grating noise, a quality of light, a tone, a habit, a nostalgia, a dream. Cannery Row is the gathered and scattered, tin and iron and rust and splintered wood, chipped pavement and weedy lots and junk heaps, sardine canneries of corrugated iron, honky tonks, restaurants and whore houses, and little crowded groceries, and laboratories and flop-houses. Its inhabitants are, as the man once said, 'whores, pimps, gamblers and sons of bitches,' by which he meant Everybody. Had the man looked through another peephole he might have said, 'Saints and angels and martyrs and holy men,' and he would have meant the same thing.

John Steinbeck, *Cannery Row,* 1945

The term *infrastructure* did not appear in everyday conversation in the United States until the mid-1950s.[2] Until then, the word had been primarily used by French military engineers. It was by way of World War I that this French military jargon infiltrated the allied vocabulary, eventually entering the English vernacular as a term indicating that which provides the means to support our way of living. Today, along with energy distribution, transportation networks, and water/sewerage systems, the term also encompasses other basic service provisions—from garbage collection and policing to public libraries and schools. It is possible to argue that infrastructure is not only responsible for our *well-being*—on a purely elemental level—but rather also for our *well-living:* including not only support of life in a physiological sense, but also in terms of culture, society, and civility.

Food growth, processing, packaging, and distribution comprise a fitting example of this development of infrastructure and its eventual evolution into "infra-culture." For while food, in principle, provides daily nourishment to individuals, food also, particularly the kind that has been specially treated to keep for a prolonged period of time, has enabled geographical exploration, trade, and war for the last several hundred years. The production of processed preserved foodstuff became highly industrialized at the end of 19th century and, by the end of World War II, had spawned a vast infrastructure of its own, spanning the original producers, preservers, the industry and science behind it, as well as delivery, advertising, and distribution systems.

But by the second half of the 20th century and now into the 21st, canned food, at least as a concept, has transformed from its original premise of basic sustenance into a cultural icon, a cultural pariah, and any combination of the above.[3] Furthermore, the idea of "canning" has transcended its original 1:1 scale. Large manifestation of the "can" containing grain, equipment, livestock, even people—Butler buildings, Quonset huts, grain silos, along with their famous derivative, the Dymaxion House, and the promise of quickly assembled prefabricated dwellings—are also part of our present physical or cultural milieu. These metamorphoses of a simple tin canister testify that we might be witnessing a transformation of infrastructure from its original "nuts and bolts" premise into a much more complex system encompassing human ecology, culture, convention, ritual, taste, and habit. Can this process, guided by exterior forces of human development, be controlled, or at least mined for its productive side-effects; and would we, the architects, as professionals particularly skilled at navigating this metamorphic "infraculture," be the ones to do it? We think yes, yes we can.

Can, the Original

Canning, like the term *infrastructure* itself, is also a French invention, again very much related to military history. In 1802, Nicholas Appert answered the call of the French government to invent a method of long-term food preservation suitable for supplying the troops engaged in the multiple wars of the young republic. Napoleon Bonaparte himself issued a reward of 12,000 francs for the processes originally called "appertizing."[4] The process is largely unchanged today—prepared food, vegetables or meats, are briefly heated before being tightly sealed into a container. Appert himself was not quite able to explain the science behind his invention, and it was only by virtue of another Frenchman, Louis Pasteur, that the role of microbes and bacteria living in our food was understood.

The real breakthrough that allowed canning to become a serious industry, giving the whole process its modern name, was the invention of the sealed, corrugated, double-seamed tin. The appearance of this container sometime in the late 1880s enabled the exploration of the most remote corners of the world, the proliferation of colonial empires, the subsequent waging of the two world wars over those colonies, as well as the Cold War, and the Moon walk.

Neverslip Solder

The Solder that Does Things

LANG'S AUTOMATIC NEVERSLIP HEMMED CAP MACHINE

Steel Can Capper

A Sure Seal Guaranteed

Lang's Neverslip Solder— The product of Orignal distinction. Just a little bit better than other **WIRE SOLDERS**

LANG'S NEVERSLIP CAP DROPPER

Buy Lang's products and stretch the earning ca= pacity of every **DOLLAR INVESTED**

LANG'S NEVERSLIP WIRE MACHINE

The man who figures factory costs and NEVERSLIPS Recommends Lang's Products

Exhibit Space No. 164 BALTIMORE CONVENTION

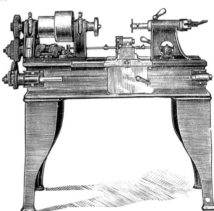

LANG'S WIRE SPOOLER

 E. M. LANG COMPANY, Portland, Maine

While it is not clear who is solely responsible for the "tin canister,"[5] this simple device provided numerous benefits: it could be produced cheaply and its contents could be preserved longer, its shape and materiality reduced shipping weight and cost, making storing/stacking a more efficient operation. The United States itself owes its initials, the *U.S.,* and its namesake Uncle Sam, to a certain Samuel Wilson of Troy, NY—a meat-packer and canner, supplier to the American army during the War of 1812. Wilson's packaging was stamped with capital letters *U* and *S,* and soldiers called the produce Uncle Sam's. Wilson also looked the part, according to his photo. In 1959, Congress made it official.

Can Transform(ed)

World War II transformed the canning industry into a highly efficient system of farming, canning plants, metal fabricators, machine shops, and delivery services in order to supply the troops overseas. At this time, the military also started experimenting with canning things other than prepared food—first on a small, and then on a much larger scale. In 1943, the U.S. Navy started shipping clothing, ammunition, and engines in large sealed tin containers in order to minimize exposure to elements and better preserve the contents. At the same time, Buckminster Fuller was commissioned to design an easily deployable housing unit, based on his original experiments on the Butler grain bin. The result was two built prototypes of the Dymaxion House. Neither ever entered production—the war, by then, was over.

Yet the original metal grain bin, patented in the 1900s, is still a persistent landmark in most rural areas of the United States. New, prefabricated metal grain bins are still available from catalogs at relatively low prices in a variety of diameters and heights, complete with engineer's drawings and step-by-step assembly instructions that will yield a complete and sound structure in a matter of days (if not hours).[6] The horizontally oriented "halved" version of the grain bin, known as the Quonset Hut, has been in development since World War I and became widespread during World War II, housing ammunitions, supplies, and troops themselves. Today, the Quonset hut is no longer in production,[7] but the few that remain have attained a cult status.

(No Model.)

E. R. PRUITT.
CANNING MACHINERY.

No. 512,323.   Patented Jan. 9. 1894.

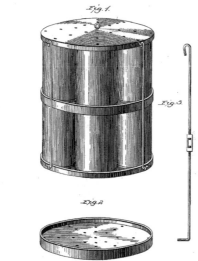

Fig.1.

Fig.3

Fig.2

Witnesses:
Harry D. Rohrer
W. Aughinbaugh

Inventor:
Eugene R. Pruitt
By J. Krebs Trunk Atty.

THE NATIONAL LITHOGRAPHING COMPANY,
WASHINGTON, D. C.

H. G. HARRISON.
GRAIN TANK.
APPLICATION FILED APR. 11, 1916.

1,242,935.   Patented Oct. 16, 1917.
2 SHEETS—SHEET 1.

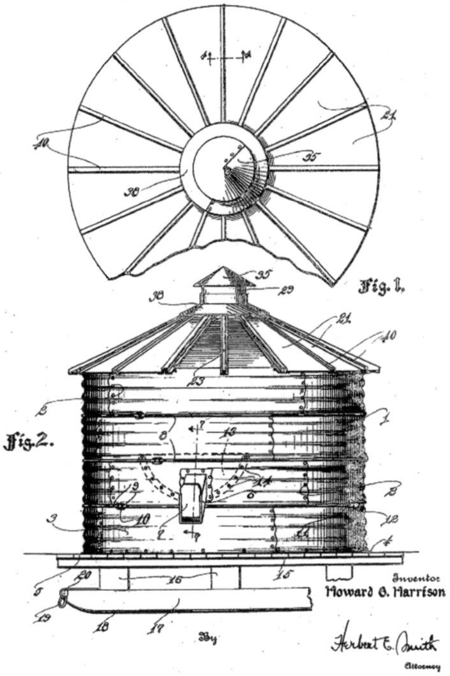

Fig.1.

Fig.2.

Inventor
Howard G. Harrison
By
Herbert E. Smith
Attorney

J. N. BALLOU & J. J. SHIRLEY.
STEEL GRAIN BIN.
(Application filed May 4, 1901.)

(No Model.)

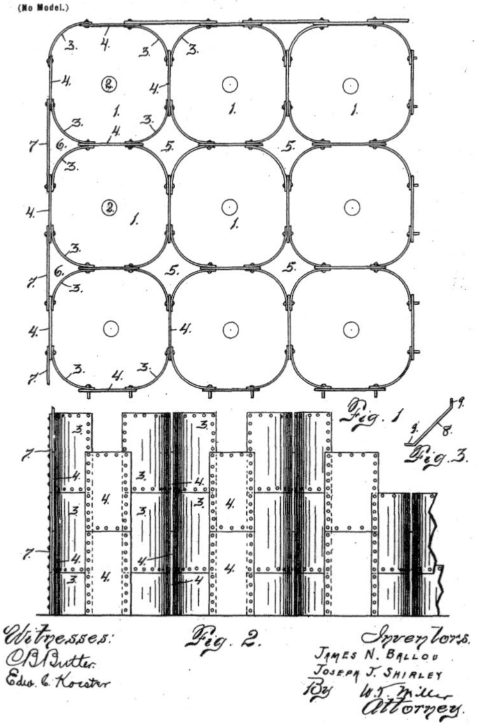

Fig.1.

Fig.2.   Fig.3.

Witnesses:
O. B. Butter
Edio C. Koester

Inventors.
James N. Ballou
Joseph J. Shirley
By W. J. Miller
Attorney.

1, 1942.   **R. B. FULLER**   Des. 133,411
PREFABRICATED HOUSE
Filed May 31, 1941

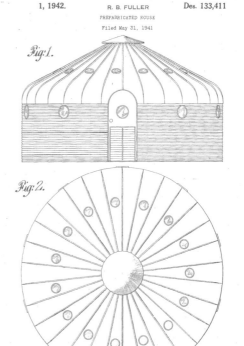

Fig:1.

Fig:2.

INVENTOR
RICHARD BUCKMINSTER FULLER
BY J. Philip Churchill
ATTORNEY

Can Now?

Since World War II, canned products have been transformed from objects of necessity into cultural phenomena. Cans of Spam and Campbell's Soup have contributed both to the demise of the Eastern Block and the reemergence of (some of) those countries as part of the Western world in the early 1990s.[8] On an individual scale, processed foods have also been implicated in transforming us physically: preservatives used in canned foods are blamed for various cancers, not to mention the obesity epidemic. We have also arrived at the point where the original premise of canning, preserving food to enable an epic journey to the far corners of the world, is largely moot, as almost any remote point can be accessed faster than food can spoil. Another side effect of canning has been the "disconnect" of food production from food consumption. While food supply is still short in many parts of the world, a vast infrastructure built around instant processed preserved food is at a point where it is no longer sustainable ecologically, economically, or ethically. Today's emphasis is on the fresh and the local, not preserved or imported: "locavores" do not do cans.

And the Future Can …

Today Steinbeck's Cannery Row is long gone. What remains is a vast network of supply, production, and delivery systems that has also outlived its intended usage. Scores of grain bins and silos dot the agrarian landscape, slowly rusting away, giving way to residential subdevelopments as food production shifts into its new paradigm. Instead of leaving the ruins behind and among us, like many other "legacy infrastructures" from the centuries of industrial boom, we wonder how some of this built-up mass that produced, packaged, marketed, and distributed a finished product can be of renewed use today and in the future. Rather than starting from scratch, knowledge and materials can be recycled—reutilizing existing tried-and-true supply and delivery methods for purposes beyond canned tuna. Furthermore, it is possible that the familiar image of this "infrastructure," along with its cultural and symbolic implications can be subverted for new rather than nostalgic purposes. There can be an evolution within the infrastructure. As political and social currents warm up, old infrastructure associated with "the ways of the past" becomes abandoned, a lesson that has been learned since antiquity. Yet also since that time, what was once "abandoned" has often become "repurposed." Consider the transformation of a roman arena into a medieval town a dozen centuries later. It is a development that is beyond the mere reutilization of brick and stone; it involves a change of scale, purpose, and societal convention, on the one hand, and direct reutilization of support system (enclosure) and a sense of place (appreciation for grandeur of a public structure), on the other hand. This simultaneous adaptation and invention normally takes a long time, but since speed and immediacy are characteristic of our time, we too imagine the possibility of "harvesting" canning, or at least certain manifestations of it, to new ends.

Consider a typical metal grain bin, 36 feet in diameter, roughly 1,000 square feet of interior footprint along with over a century[9] of amassed knowledge and technology associated with it. The production capacity that is associated with manufacturing, engineering, delivery, and assembly of these structures is truly impressive—within days, a new building, immune not only to weather outside, but also to certain internal stresses and gravity, can be erected virtually anywhere. It is extremely durable, efficient, and inexpensive. There is a clear need for cheap quickly assembled structures for housing, storage, and even productive gardens on sites of earthquakes, landslides, brownfields, and so on that would allow displaced communities to be instrumental in supporting their own livelihoods. At a time when housing, both as emergency shelter and permanent construction, is a pressing issue across the globe, a metal grain bin, as an almost instant prefabricated housing solution, could be an attractive option. But in the last century, hundreds of patents on prefab houses were granted, and none of them made it into mass production precisely because they were lacking the manufacturing base associated with sourcing, fabrication, engineering, and delivery. In short, they lacked the fundamental infrastructure of a simple grain bin.

Apparently, the same appeal existed in 1943, when Buckminster Fuller's Dymaxion House was commissioned. The premise was beautiful: prefabricated metal shell, utilizing the excess of the military industrial complex, coupled with a passive ventilation system based on natural air flow noted to exist in a grain drier, combined with a prefabricated monocoque bathroom unit that was originally designed to be water-free.[10] Even though the infrastructural consideration was met, the house failed to enter into mass production. Much speculation exists on the Dymaxion failure: ultimately, the masterful consideration of "infrastructure" was simply not enough. It failed to consider the larger issue of "infraculture."

To the builders or the clientele of the suburban housing (at least in the United States), the failures of Dymaxion House and its "nonnormative" prefab brethren are quite apparent. One might ask: How do I live in a circle if my favorite couch, my kitchen table, and my armoire are rectangles? Why does my house not look like a "real house"? Why does it not look like the houses over in the next town? Will I be able to sell it? Will the others like it, even if I do? As primitive as they may appear, these are perhaps the most fundamental questions when it comes to housing: economics and aesthetics, tethered together in this mysterious notion of "curb appeal. "From the standpoint of local zoning codes and ordinances, "prefab" is not even considered on par with "real" housing and would more likely be relegated to a trailer park than be allowed in a "good neighborhood," citing lack of response and appreciation of the established residential context; in other words, again, the failure to uphold the curb appeal. Furthermore, even though prefab carries the promise of independence from local house builders and developers, this does not entirely hold true. Since building and zoning codes vary, regulating not only the appearance but, more importantly, delivery and connection of utilities, local contractors necessarily will be involved, at least in the foundation, mechanical, electrical, and plumbing work. And local builders and developers, ever sensitive to the balance of market forces and construction means, have devised a certain way of working that is tightly keyed both into the concept of curb appeal, and numerous other pragmatic considerations, such as market demand and construction materials, their sizes, prices, and availability. And fundamentally, construction loans, the financing and lending industry, fuel developers and builders alike. Lending parameters are defined by local real estate comparables and driven primarily by cumbersome assessment formulas as mysterious as the notion of curb appeal itself, resulting in a system in which prefabricated housing is not at all equally represented. More than 50 years of this paradigm has resulted in a fascinating amalgam of innovation and regression, manifested formally in the homogeneous suburban landscape with oversized and underused

housing stock—extremely efficient in the way it is built and extremely conservative in its appearance. The consequence is one that allows a very small margin of
deviation formally and, therefore, structurally and materially.

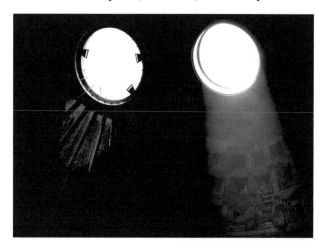

Can Exterior

Now, nearly 70 years after Bucky's Dymaxion House, how might we begin to reconsider canned architecture? First, consider that the grain bin is not a foreign object and as such exists as a domestic infrastructure capable of its own role within the cultural milieu—as a signifier of country living. Metal grain bins continue to dot the American landscape; by now they are more symbolic of the pastoral farm of yore than a functional piece of agrarian infrastructure. Yet these structures transcend that symbolic role, for while often preserved as storage sheds, they have on occasion emerged as bespoke residences. This may take care of curb appeal: it is no longer a foreign entity, but rather a familiar, and increasingly more desired, sight. Along with an abstract image of a "house" (with a pitched roof) as a concept of domesticity, the grain bin can begin to conjure an image of farm living, a version of the American Gothic, albeit with a hint of industry, ingenuity, and innovation. Considered as an enclosure system, it is efficient and structurally sound—and builders would appreciate the possibility of erecting an enclosed structure cheaply, within days, in order to spend time on the interior build-out without being subjected to seasonal limitations of construction. Furthermore, as a function of quantity of material, the round exterior yields minimal perimeter and maximum enclosure, ultimately promising energy efficiency. Now that the age of the McMansion is over, the possibility of the expeditious erection of the house perimeter seems to be a more productive priority than its apparent opposite: maximum lot coverage with a single-story structure. This new way of living aligns with a readjustment in a new financial context and awareness of excess consumption.

Can Interior

The idea of inhabiting rotund spaces has a particular place in history of architecture—for it is often associated with exceptional, abnormal, elevated, or ceremonial circumstance—everything that is the very opposite of "domestic." The ancients preferred to bury their dead within circles—numerous rotund tombs dot Via Apia Antica in Rome—and to this day the tombs remain. Castel Sant'Angelo (née Hadrian's mausoleum) is an example of the repurposing of the infrastructure of the dead for that of the living. But at the time of the conversion of this tomb into a papal fortress, the idea of platonic shapes and their connection with the human body was being (re)discovered. Circles became appealing again. By the late Renaissance and beyond, the grandeur of a circular structure was further domesticated into Palladian villas, and eventually made its way into almost all corners of the old and new world.[11] Here, with a few modifications, it entered the American highbrow vernacular in Monticello, and even further, to the Oval Office in the White *House* (where the president sits at a rectangular desk).

After some flirtation with the rotund and the freeform in the 20th century,[12] the cylinders today remain largely unwelcome on a domestic scale. The problem is inevitable: a round hole into which square pegs of furniture and other domestic accoutrements must be inserted. In the past, within the architecture design studios (in this esteemed institution and beyond), certain colloquial terms were developed to describe various spatial conditions of a plan—such as the fried egg (referring to a well-defined figure on the interior and a flexible, porous perimeter). Perhaps it is time to introduce another term—a breakfast of two soft-boiled eggs, for example, referring specifically to the "can condition," where both the rigid perimeter and the flexible interior can be addressed in the academic setting.

And in its new manifestation, the grain bin (or cluster of grain bins, à la the six pack) can become a canister for storing the humanoid, her possessions, her partner, and her pets, as well as all of their systems of *well-being* and concepts of *well-living*—without losing sight of the American Dream of a single and detached dwelling in the landscape. This newly conceived can allows a reengagement with history, ecology, and society of the American landscape. It can provide for the residents' civility toward themselves, as well as toward those who came before, through ingenious reuse; and those who will come after, by resourceful management of materials and resources. Perhaps this will constitute an essence in the creation of sustainable infrastructure, in which we, the people (and architects), can play a central role.

Endnotes

1 http://www.epa.gov/waste/nonhaz/municipal/pubs/msw2008rpt.pdf.
2 A search in the *New York Times* archives reveals that phenomenon.
3 For an example of cultural iconography, witness the original tin can in the Museum of Modern Art's Design section, as well as silk screens by Andy Warhol. As an example of canned food as a cultural pariah, consider Spam. Last, consider the Soviet Ministry of Culture denouncing Andy Warhol's art as "anti-Soviet" while distributing cans of Spam as "food bonuses" to its employees.
4 This version of the invention of food conservation process is embraced by the American Canning Association—and can be found in its annual publications.
5 Several U.S. and British patents were issued around the same time.
6 Though demand in the United States is low, most of the steel bin manufacturers refocus on overseas markets (i.e., Russia, China, and Latin America) or attempt at advertising their product for other purposes (i.e., general storage).
7 Though it spawned a whole industry of agrarian metal buildings. See http://www.ussteelbuildings.com.
8 In the late 1980s various Western food containers started to penetrate the iron curtain. While their contents were consumed, the containers themselves became venerated objects of desire: they were traded, repurposed, reused, or even simply displayed in people's homes as artifacts from the other, foreign, world.
9 Patented around 1900.
10 The early conception of Dymaxion House is described in Beatriz Colomina's *Domesticity at War* (MIT Press, 2007).
11 In the year that the world celebrated Andrea Palladio's 500th birthday, we would like to put forward the idea that his *Quattro Libri* is singlehandedly responsible for the proliferation of the roman circle in the world.
12 Consider, on the one hand, Le Corbusier and the idea of the free plan; and on the other hand, Konstantin Melnikov, with his 1926 house in Moscow—a twinned cylinder system that was developed as a prototype for efficient worker housing.

Dear Ila,

In a recent lecture at the Future of Design Conference at the University of Michigan, you spoke about the changing relationship between nature and culture and the role that recycled materials might play in the future of our discipline. You predict that "we will encounter the inversion of our modern obsession with production and consumption through the digestion and regeneration of objects; the other of production is the disassembly/reassembly process."

We invite you to elaborate on the ideas of digestion and regeneration, and the implications of these processes within a consumerist society, with respect to contemporary practices in art, architecture, and urbanism.

—Eds.

Trash versus Operations, Fresh Kills Park project,
James Corner Field Operations.

Ila Berman

is an architect, theorist and director of architecture at California College of the Arts (CCA). Berman's work and publications include the book URBANbuild local global, New Orleans: Strategies for a City in Soft Land, *"Amphibious Territories" in AD and the Urban Mappings for a Future City exhibition at the 2006 International Architectural Biennale in Venice.*

Regenerative Returns

One of the most dominant themes in contemporary architectural practice is the new and expanding relationship being generated between nature and culture. As digital practices emulate living models and animate patterns of biological growth, and as green landscape ecologies are routinely called on to cloak the surfaces of the future urban agropolis, smooth mixtures are emerging everywhere that render ambiguous the traditional opposition of nature and culture, the biotic and the mechanistic. This newly acculturated nature is the product of highly technological practices, yet is directly linked to the primordial by its affinities with the complexity of living systems and the continuities of "raw" unformed matter. In cultural artifacts, the continuous material and experiential field deemed intrinsic to the natural world, is divided into discrete signifiers, representational figures, and formal percepts—to render value to matter, and attribute to it a framework for human intelligibility, perception, and use. Nature is continuous, whereas culture is inherently discrete. This division, which precedes the construction of our own individuation and subjectivity, is the means by which we instrumentalize the real, and transform matter into useful and meaningful cultural artifacts. We cannot, therefore, enter into a discussion of current architectural practices without realizing that they have radically transformed, as biotechnologies have, these traditional distinctions; and we must attempt to understand the consequences of this new synthetic nature.

Indeed, despite both our real and symbolic fascination with the natural, as evident in all of its abundant architectural forms (perhaps at the very moment that we fear its disappearance), the ever-increasing domination of organics by technics and the depletion of natural ecologies is still one of the prevailing issues facing our global culture. Many have argued, including Caroline Merchant in *The Death of Nature,* and Herbert Marcuse in *One Dimensional Man,* that the pervasiveness of the technological, which entails the appropriation of all natural matter, effectuates our own absorption into, and potential domination by, the very technologies of our own creation.[1] According to Marcuse, this is the inevitable result of the absolute coordination of the ideational and empirical in a world governed by technological reason, for which the regimented and functionalized space of modern industry (intrinsically linked up with modern science, on the one hand, and modern capitalism, on the other hand) has become the paradigmatic example. Under the technological a priori of this regime, Marcuse states that the primary material of nature, inclusive of all forms of organic life, is conceptualized only as "potential instrumentality, stuff of control and organization." In the tradition of Western progress, nature is thereby appropriated as a resource for the artificial production of culture, where fundamentally the "instrumentalization of things" also presupposes the "instrumentalization of man."[2]

In his analysis of the epistemological shift that occurred at the emergence of the modern, Foucault describes the historic role that architecture has fulfilled within this regime as a regulatory mechanism and disciplinary machine employed to correct and control the operations of the body. The factory, which was advanced as the explicit prototypical model of architectural order, functional efficiency, and social regulation, was thus a means to not only transform matter into usable artifacts, but also to efficiently instrumentalize its occupants—to produce a utilitarian body, at once obedient and useful, to be molded according to precise functional programs within rigidly defined architectural spaces of geometric clarity.[3] By the beginning of the 21st century, despite having moved far beyond the reified mechanistic models described by Gideon and the ideological terrain of Taylorism, the ever-increasing proliferation and permeation of technologies into our daily lives is seemingly indisputable. The greatest single effect of this saturation is that it has transformed us all into cyborgs, synthetic hybrids of machine and organism, the boundaries of which have become increasingly precarious.[4] Two decades ago, Donna Haraway had written that, within the contemporary world, the cyborg is both the most disturbing and the most real and ubiquitous, rendering fragile the constitution of humanity and the threshold of the natural. "Late twentieth-century machines have made thoroughly ambiguous the difference between natural and artificial, mind and body, self-developing and externally designed, and many other distinctions that used to apply to organisms and machines. Our machines are disturbingly lively, and we ourselves frighteningly inert."[5] Yet for Haraway, the cyborg was not a lamentable fact of the postindustrial world, but rather a space of potential political subversion, cautioning that it is necessary to avoid the double pitfall of the either/or response to technology: either blindly accepting technological determinism, or resolutely resisting it by becoming a pre-technological Luddite. Instead, her political response was intended to recall us to an imagined organicism and to integrate our resistance (drawing from Merchant and Marcuse), yet to critically and strategically engage the world of technological mediation as a productive and political imperative, in a way, however, that might rethink and redirect its energies in support of the living.[6]

It is certainly clear that many current architectural practices are attempting to do precisely this, and that our revived fascination with the "living" and the desire to establish new linkages across the nature-culture divide has been one of the strongest trajectories we have encountered in recent years, despite the fact that the design territories and approaches that have been developed are as diverse as the natural systems they seem to emulate. The proliferation of morphogenetic evolutionary methodologies that simulate generative patterns of continuous form growth and development through computational geometries, represent an entire spectrum of strategies, each of which reconnects the technological with the organic territory from which it was separated, by drawing dynamic material logics back into the cultural artifact.[7] The artificially entangled life forms of R&Sie(n) Architects—from the invaginated intricate geometries of *I've Heard About,* to the fuzzy aggregates of *Olzweg*—create intensively material dystopic environments that undermine the definition of the cultural object, while establishing new forms of random self-generation whose modes of emergence and behavior refer more to biotic animate beings than to the technologies responsible for their very creation.

I've Heard About 2005, R&Sie(n), François Roche,
Stephanie Lavaux, with Stephan Henrich.

In the many experimental design studios of Francois Roche and Mark Fornes,
we are again confronted with intelligent forms of so-called primitive materiality,
each of which defines a new relationship with the machinic.

Opus 2008, Francois Roche Studio GSAPP, Inviting
Marc Fornes, Chi Chen Yang Student.

Akin to Roxy Paine's technologically manufactured and overtly codified red "scumaks," these biomachinic matters seem to render us all primitive cyborgs, extremely technologically proficient yet intensely and euphorically immersed in the primordial flux of matter and its experience. Aranda/Lasch's Grotto project, Kokkugia's ongoing research into wetFoam geometries, and MOS's growing Ivy project,

Grotto, Aranda\Lasch, PS-I Entry 2005.   **Algorithmic Wet Foam Study**, Kokkugia.

for example, each establish analogical links to continuous and transformative natural material landscapes directly resulting from the intricate patterns of their evolutionary emergence.

Although specifically distinct in their operations and effects, in all of these new "natures," Foucault's modern architectural disciplinary machines are seemingly replaced by vital, biomachinic matters. This "machinic phylum,"[8] simultaneously artificial in its production and natural in affect, not only establishes a new continuum traversing the culture-nature dichotomy, but also inverts the traditional modern hierarchy, such that technologies are now being employed to amplify, register, and reveal, rather than constrain and functionalize, the dynamic potentials of animate matter.

Nature's clouds, flocks, swarms, and termite mounds have become paradigmatic models for those intent on rethinking architecture as a dynamic transformation of collective biotic material. From The Living's underwater *Amphibious Architecture* installation (which enables us to communicate with urban fish) to their *Living Light* project, a dynamic responsive skin that registers urban air quality in Seoul, Korea, our expanded culture-nature interface has also enabled the insertion of a protean environmental wilderness and feedback loop into architecture's domestic terrain. Beyond dissolving the boundary between human and animal territories, a condition that Haraway cites as a marker potentially linking ecological awareness with urban mythologies,[9] these practices point to another environmental response to postindustrialization, where technology's apparent physical absence—its disappearance into the "atmospheric"—has prompted architectural territories to be transformed into ambient meteorological events. In our world of digitized information and intelligent matters, our explorations of ambient and atmospheric environments, those defined by fluid continuous qualities rather than the discrete delimitation of defined objects, have called into question architecture's cultural role as a provider of spatial stability and material permanence. Interactive responsive fields, such as the early digitized *Flux* room installation by Reiser + Umemoto, or the more recent *White Noise/White Light* field by Howeler + Yoon, sited at the base of the Acropolis in Athens,

Flux Room, RUR Architecture.

White Noise/White Light, Howeler and Yoon, Photo: Andy Ryan.

generate animate "atmospheres" that respond to their living occupation.

In these projects, emergent environments are not the result of morphogenetic operations, but rather the result of interactive programming embedded into the potential functioning of the space, such that its affects are dynamically revealed and experienced by direct engagement and immersion. Responsive systems are used to express the choreography of inhabitation through the filter of an interactive gradient field in continual flux. These are technologized spatial environments employed to amplify (rather than constrain) the gestural excesses of animate biotic behaviors, or in the case of Omar Kahn's *Open Columns Project,* for example, to provide a changing material index of the composite biochemical and gaseous by-products of human inhabitation. Architecture is deployed as an infrastructure that organizes the variable spectra of potential material responses and that dynamically stimulates and enables the expressive production of a multitude of artificial atmospheric effects.

Our strange fascination with these new artificial "natures" in their many distinct forms—seemingly symbolic compensatory acts that repeat our return to the discovery and exploitation of new "virgin" territories—often remain somewhat impotent when examined according to the performance of these projects in relation to actual living systems. We are acutely aware of the fact that the architectural emulation of growing, animate, or atmospheric environments as an investigation of new modes of architectural form generation or the material amplification and expression of its ambient affects, do not, despite their biomimetic appeal or communicative engagement, contribute in any fundamental way to the enhancement of real nature or the mitigation of its cultural instrumentalization. Conversely, those on the other side of the nature-culture continuum, who have been developing systemic explorations into energy-generating, bioremediating, and recyclable materials and systems (the environmentally "responsible," rather than environmentally "affected"), although certainly not influenced by geometries that emulate natural formation or its primordial sensual affects, are overtly concerned with natural material, biological and chemical processes; yet where the material functions of these processes have often had little effect on the actual form generation, spatial disposition, or symbolic intentions—that is, the design—of the biodegradable artifacts they produce. The widening gap between those focused on creative formal, morphological, experiential, and interactive processes and those whose emphasis is on material technologies and their ecological functioning, exposes the lamentable segregations still evident in our design thinking. Despite the pervasiveness of our symbolic return to nature, the seemingly endless appropriation and instrumentalization of the natural world for the surplus products of culture, still reigns within the postindustrial and postcapitalist regimes within which we are operating. Against the backdrop of global warming and extreme environmental depletion, our absorption into this web has taken on a new urgency, foregrounding our own biological fragility within the context of the post-natural cyborgian future we have already created.

Perhaps one of the greatest future challenges that will dominate the design industry is initiating the inversion and integration of these principles, through the reduction, transformation, and recycling of cultural waste concurrent with the design and construction of newly acculturated natures in many different forms. Just as steel, concrete, and glass were the new homogeneous materials to represent the industrialization of 20th-century modernity, and plastics signified the utopian trajectory of the 1960s, for our postmillennial future, in addition to the continued development of new biotechnological materials, one of the most important raw materials for design will be trash. Our future return to matter, will therefore not only be through the sensuous deployment of form and the atmospheric extension of design, but also through something far more primitive—the ways in which we generate new processes that collect, sort, filter, pulverize, mix, melt, and modulate trash. Currently our largest renewable resource, trash will become our new postindustrial nature and future raw matter—an inherently heterogeneous mixture whose modes of typological and functional classification will be simultaneously determined by biological and technological properties. Within the context of this postnatural "real," our framework for authenticity and origins is dissolved, as the endlessness of nature's transformative operations are drawn on as models for cultural production, and as biotechnologically regenerated trash—a new form of raw repotentialized postaccultured matter—becomes the substantive material matrix for future design endeavors.

Despite the obvious fact that our current deleterious environmental impacts would be substantially reduced if we simply manufactured, built, used, and disposed of less—a concept that undermines the impulse toward excessive production that drives global capitalism—the true inversion of our modern obsession with production and consumption is not only to be found in their absence (for those who yearn toward a preindustrial future), but rather in their much needed reversal, by amplifying processes and designs that contribute to cultural digestion and regeneration. The "other" of production, therefore, refers not only to a redefinition of consumption that expands the parameters of both use and design, but also to the inversion of production through an emphasis on the disassembly reassembly process—an evolutionary, ecotechnological model of regeneration that would require that we spend as much of our energy on the strategic recycling of matter, form, and space as we do on the creative design of new objects. William McDonough's proposition to incorporate the concept of biological and technological nutrients into our design parameters to transform the way we think about materiality (his now famous dictum: "waste = food") is one strategy for ensuring that the physical substance of cultural products have the potential to be biologically "digested" when literally buried in landfills, or infinitely recycled when returned as secondary materials for industrial reprocessing.[10] In spite of the questionable application of intensive ecological strategies directed toward products, such as cars, seemingly by their very nature ecologically irresponsible artifacts, McDonough's model U Ford concept car (2003), one of many new proposals for hydrogen-fueled electric hybrid vehicles, incorporated modular disassembly methods and plant-based manufacturing materials as a way of integrating digestive and regenerative strategies into the design process. Biopolymers such as polylactide (PLA) fabrics derived from corn- as well as soy-based foam, and machined components used in its design ensured the potential biodegradability of parts of its vehicular apparatus while engendering new biotechnological continuities between cultural and natural systems. If, for Frank Lloyd Wright, it was the car, through its freedom of access, that enabled us to directly engage the expansiveness of the natural landscape, for McDonough, it seems we should also be transported by a biotic digestible trace of this landscape's very constitution.

Although the history of material recycling through design has offered us many trajectories—from the redeployment of cardboard and chain link (symbolically loaded cheap "secondary" materials) in the early work of Frank Gehry, to the human nest chair made of scrap fabric of Emily Pillotin, or the entangled mesh of waste plastic of the RD4 chairs by Richard Liddle/Cohda design, few of these projects imagine the temporal, spatial, and material afterlife of their own disassembly, digestion, and regeneration. In addition, the difference in impulse between the ad hoc forms of recycling that dominated the fragmented collaged works of the 1980s and 90s and our current trajectories, exposes the direct influence that both the rapid expansion of biological and digital technologies have had on our understanding of digestive and regenerative processes. Even our current processes of design, often modeled on incremental evolutionary operations that either emulate forms of artificial life through genetic coding or digitally recycle existing contexts by generating continuities from the fragments or pixilated "bits" of disparate cultural systems, seem to be cultural extensions of natural modes of organic recycling. It is as though we are fulfilling some strange ecological or evolutionary imperative. Unlike their earlier Frankensteinian counterparts, these more recent forms of synthetic nature have emerged from a technological primordial soup, seemingly an aftereffect of the now-digitized compost pile of culture.

Perhaps the most compelling of regenerative design strategies to emerge are those that operate on the urban and territorial scales, from disciplines such as landscape architecture that have traditionally incorporated living matter into the design process and that are having the largest influence on urban bioremediation and geographical recycling. In projects such as *Lifescape,* Field Operation's proposal for Fresh Kills, one of the largest landfill landscapes in existence, 150 million tons of human cultural waste have literally become the base material for a new living landscape ecology. Now referred to as the Fresh Kills Reserve (in a strange oxymoronic twist), the project proposes a regenerative strategy that will intensify natural wildlife by exploiting the biotic potential of its estuarine geomorphology while reconnecting it to its newly colonized postnatural alien ecology, with diverse cultural and recreational programming intended for human inhabitation. As the nature-culture trajectory is inverted, the redefinition and recycling of the landfill as lifescape, and the direct amplification of strategies intended to augment living systems through networks—threads, surface mats, and clusters—that redistribute flows of water, energy, and matter across the site and ensure its requisite porosity and protection, are indicative of a design trajectory that is modeled on principles of regeneration and whose formal, spatial, and material strategies are active embodiments of the processes it supports.

In addition, projects within urban design such as the *Growing Water* project, designed by the Chicago Urban Lab for the City of the Future competition, recycles wastewater, infrastructure, and space through an integrated matrix of "Eco-Boulevards" that link local biospheres to larger regional and global ecologies. Drawing from the ecological engineering research of biologist John Todd, this project proposes to use "living machines"[11]—those that literally incorporate biotic vegetation and organisms such as microbes, plants, algae, fish, and snails into cultural reprocessing systems—to phytoremediate 100 percent of Chicago's wastewater without toxic chemicals, while harvesting and recircuiting its regenerated and purified liquid products for reconsumption. This and other projects—such as *Urban Aeration* by Konyk Architecture, generated for the d3 Natural Systems Competition—that integrate permeable carbon-capturing material filtration mechanisms to recycle urban toxins, or the *Living Tower* project by SOA, that establishes new territories for urban and architectural syntheses intended to limit the eco-footprint of our farming practices by incorporating them into high-density urban agricultural communities, focus on the syntheses of architectural, urban, and landscape practices to recycle and revivify space while limiting the natural devastation that results from sprawl and geographical consumption.

It would seem that we need to allow for a new expanded understanding of what a postindustrial culture-nature continuum might entail in relation to design—one that is much more aware of the larger cultural, spatial, material, and temporal cycles that influence the life of the objects and architectures that we produce. There is certainly a necessity to synthetically integrate biotic materials and technologies, or methods for disassembly and reassembly (intended as exchangeable/recyclable products of service),[12] into our culturally informed design strategies, yet these are only meaningful when understood within a broader cultural and environmental context. Even the "digestible" solar-powered mini-mobile device of the future must be imagined in both spatial and material terms, and respond to the temporal microcycle of its design, manufacture, and use, in relation to the much longer macrocycle required for its biodegradation (or a more immediate cycle of disassembly and technological regeneration), if we are to truly reverse or redirect current trajectories and productively relink them to a larger biotic material matrix. The questionable demand for the physical durability of our everyday cultural artifacts remains, for example, if the speed of design fashion (dependent on uniqueness and high-velocity turnover), capitalist overproduction (dependent on quantity), and technological innovation, are not equally retooled according to parameters that redirect their energies in support of the living, lest we transform the earth and all of the life forms it supports into one enormous sacrificial landscape. Perhaps it will be only when we begin to comprehend the evolution of our own forms of cultural production in terms of the complexity of nature's systemic ecologies that will we truly initiate the inversion required for our own regenerative return.

Endnotes

1 See Caroline Merchant, *The Death of Nature* (New York: HarperCollins, 1980) and Herbert Marcuse, *One Dimensional Man* (Boston: Beacon, c1964, 1991).

2 Marcuse writes that "[s]cientific rationality makes for a specific societal organization precisely because it projects mere form (or mere matter—here, the otherwise opposite terms converge) which can be bent to practically all ends. Formalization and functionalization are, prior to all application, the pure form of a concrete societal practice. While science freed men from the 'natural' hierarchy of personal dependence and related them to each other in accordance with quantifiable qualities—namely as units of abstract labor power, calculable in units of time. By virtue of the rationalization of the modes of labor, the elimination of qualities is transferred from the universe of science to that of daily experience." Herbert Marcuse, *One Dimensional Man,* 154–159.

3 Michel Foucault, "Docile Bodies," in *Discipline and Punish: The Birth of the Prison,* Alan Sheridan (trans.) (London: Allen Lane, 1972).

4 Donna Haraway, "A Manifesto for Cyborgs," in *Simians, Cyborgs, and Women: The Reinvention of Nature* (New York: Routledge, 1990), 150.

5 Ibid., 152.

6 Ibid.

7 In addition to those cited, see Evan Douglis, *Autogenic Structures* (New York: Taylor & Francis, 2009).

8 On the "machinic phylum," see Gilles Deleuze and Félix Guattari, *A Thousand Plateaus,* Brian Massumi (trans.) (Minneapolis: University of Minnesota, 1987), 410 and 510–514.

9 See Haraway, Ibid., 151–152. "By the late twentieth century in the United States scientific culture, the boundary between human and animal is thoroughly breached…. Movements for animal rights (ecological awareness) are not irrational denials of human uniqueness; they are clear-sighted recognition of connection across the discredited breach of nature and culture. Biology and evolutionary theory over the last two centuries have simultaneously produced modern organisms as objects of knowledge and reduced the line between humans and animals to a faint trace re-etched in ideological struggle or professional disputes between life and social sciences…. The cyborg appears in myth precisely where the boundary between human and animal is transgressed."

10 William McDonough and Michael Braungart, *Cradle to Cradle: Remaking the Way We Make Things* (New York: North Point Press, 2002), 92–117.

11 See Nancy Jack Todd and John Todd, *From Eco-Cities to Living Machines: Principles of Ecological Design* (Berkeley, CA: North Atlantic Books, 1994).

12 *Products of Service* is a term that refers to the replacement of ownership of objects with those that would be rented out for a limited period, defined by the product's useable lifespan, that could then be returned to the manufacturer for product, component, or material recycling. The product of service can be disassembled and regenerated, where the intention is to establish a closed loop that is defined by the technological metabolism of the object. See McDonough and Braungart, ibid., 109–115.

Mark Jarzombek

is professor of the history and theory of architecture and the associate dean of the School of Architecture and Planning at MIT. Between 1987 and 1995 he taught at Cornell University, where he edited and advised earlier issues of The Cornell Journal of Architecture.

ECO-POP

In Praise of Irony, Hyperbole, and Readymades

In the last 10 years, Sustainability and Form have dominated architectural discourse, trapping the discipline between utopian play-acting—promising what it cannot deliver—and computerized "gaming" of design extremism. *Culture,* if one can use that word, has been more or less abandoned, taken over by the preservationists and vernacuralists, not known for their theoretical elasticity and design creativity. The result is a dead zone at the center of architectural discourse. To make matters worse, no one seems to have noticed that words like *nature, city, landscape,* and even *architecture* have become ever more ambiguous and ineffective. We continue to use these words, of course, but they are holdovers from a distant past. Concepts like "Department of Architecture," and "Department of Urban Planning" are atavisms. Why should the Greek word *architectos* and the Latin world *urbs* still seem relevant even after some 2,000 years of history? And certainly the Latin *natura* is by now nothing more than a shifting—if not actually an empty—signifier. Architects who present "green buildings" with blue skies and leafy trees seem not to have noticed that the Enlightenment equation of social harmony and verdant nature is dead.

Further, in the 1990s, the study of culture as its own "construction" began to disappear as a subject of study in the schools of architecture—creating the split we have today between form and preservation, between a mythology of endless choice and a pathology of timeless permanence. It is in the context of this disappearance-of-culture in the schools of architecture that we have seen the rise of Sustainability and Parametrics.

I do not lament the loss of culture and the death nature within the field of architecture, but state it as a given. Architecture must ultimately *accept* its fate as a disciple of uncertainty and to this end we must engage (or perhaps reengage) architecture as play of concepts—living or dead.

ECO-POP is the design strategy that embraces *both* our untenable cultural predicament *and* the vacuity of the idea of nature. It allows us to move away from our obsession with designer objects toward ready-made realities. ECO-POP, however, is not about design-from-below; it does not attempt to give voice to the "nonarchitectural" community. Its goal is rather to think outside of the conventional "design" ethos and make use of cultural productions, tropes, and critiques that may not require "design" themselves, but that can be grafted *into* the processes of architecture.

In the large map of our discourse, ECO-POP can, therefore, be positioned at the opposite end of parametric-driven architecture, which has extended in recent years the modernist fantasy of expertise over the dead body of culture.

ECO-POP hopes to expose computational architecture as little more than an attempt to keep alive the myth of animism. ECO-POP does not seek to salvage beauty in the body of the machine, but accepts the productions of culture without over-determined aesthetic presuppositions.

ECO-POP promotes alternate cultural productions to erode the persistent bond between "architecture" and "architect."

ECO-POP seeks the truth of rupture over the myths of continuity.

POP by itself is insufficient without the ECO. Architecture must embrace—perhaps go so far as to declare—the death of nature in *everything* that it does. This has to be achieved before—not after—we address the so-called ecological problems of our age. ECO-POP serves this purpose by shifting the focus from the technological to the philosophical. "Nature" is being filtered through the vortices of our cultural imaginaries, which means that architects need to wake up to these cultural constructions or be left holding an empty promise of relevancy. ECO-POP looks not past our cultural predicament but *at* it. It does not produce the empty signifier and mislabel it as "meaning" (as sustainability does), but accepts the empty signifier that is at the core of the cultural production of "nature."

There is very little history to ECO-POP, but perhaps, on the POP side of the equation, one could cite the Chiat/Day Building, Los Angeles (1985–91) by Frank Gehry. Rarely do we talk about this building today, but one can hardly overlook its rather amazing binoculars. And if the Oldenburg tactics are not enough, one is struck by the oddly aligned "sticks" holding up the roof. There was a time when tactical exaggerations and borrowings were considered a legitimate part of an architectural way of thinking, but for various reasons this approach died.

The Urban Cactus of UCX with Ben Huygen and Jasper Jaegers seems to move toward the ideas of ECO-POP. Unlike the other projects of UCX—which should be categorized as rather uninteresting examples of modernist reductionism—this building with its tree-laden curved balconies seems playful. But is it ECO-POP? No. Unfortunately the UCX architects did not consult with Natalie Jeremijenko, who not only heals "Polar Ice Cap Stress Disorder," but also plants trees upside down, as part of her TreeLogic exhibition a Mass MOCA. The trees survive quite nicely.

Her project asks us to think about our manipulations of nature while at the same time showing us an extreme example of the non-natural.

As it is, the UCX project is little more than a tower with bourgeois balcony plantings. The architects, in other words, have caved into the naive notion of nature as an ideal, though constructed, landscape for the wealthy. In accepting the status quo, they do not challenge us to rethink our attitudes toward nature. Obviously, nature is constructed—that has been true for more than 200 years. But how do we engage that construction and turn it on its head? This is what Jeremijenko does, more than literally. Her upside down trees ask us to think through our expectations. Had UCX really wanted to challenge the architectural cliché of photoshopped nature, they would have followed Jeremijenko's idea and hung the trees upside down.

The Naha Harbor Diner in Naha City Japan does more to challenge our concept of nature by redefining the role of the "tree" in architecture. The project was designed by Takeshi Hazama and built by the engineering firm Kuniken Ltd.[1] There is some difficulty in knowing what to call it, but I will insist on calling it a building. Even so, the project would hardly earn a passing grade in a design studio, despite the relatively sophisticated engineering that went into its construction.[2] The tree's bark, for example, was made of painted fiberglass-reinforced panels supported by light-gage steel frames. Hazama created small cracks in the panels and inserted mats and plants so that moss could grow from the branches. Eighty thousand small lighting fixtures were also installed on the tree's skin and restaurant facade. At night, these lights illuminate and define the shape of the tree.

This unexpected pairing of nature and artifice is extraordinarily provocative, especially as an alternative to the seductive tree romance of the film *Avatar,* which I see as merely extending the heroic, animistic fantasy of a computational fusion between man and nature. The Naha Harbor tree plays on the difference between "natural" and "manmade." It is not a conventional tree-house either, but has a modern—and rather absurdly typical—concrete building montaged into the branches.

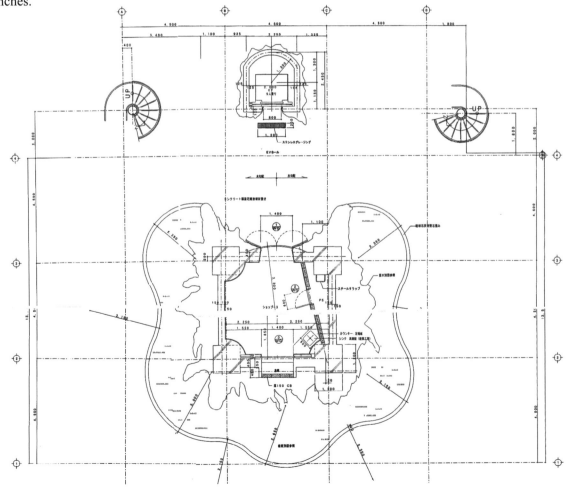

This syntactical fracture, in which both the tree and the restaurant are in quotes, is the key to this building's success. The design does not hide the restaurant in the tree, but launches it implausibly into its upper reaches, as if swept there by a great tsunami.

The disparate imaginaries out of which the diner is designed are readymades, but by putting them together, the project undermines the presumption that aesthetic production has to be an extension of the superego.

More can be done to expose the transitory state of the cultural product. We should, therefore, take the Naha Harbor Diner one step further. I propose to rebuild it next to Gehry's Stata Center designed for MIT along Vassar Street in Cambridge. The Stata Center, after all, is itself a replication of the Gehry brand. So if architects copy their own work, and corporations utilize the franchise model, why are we in the discipline of architecture so insistent on our principles of authenticity and autonomy? Such insistence has long since been obliterated as a cultural model and survives almost exclusively in the schools of architecture. The new Vassar Street tree is, however, neither brand nor franchise, but an alien insertion—a photoshop—that happily exposes the death of the *architectos* and the related death of *nature,* both of which are dialectically invisible in Gehry's building. The Vassar Street Diner will remind us that the death of these concepts is the *only* theoretical platform on which architecture can legitimately operate. The new fiberglass tree is the future set against the backdrop of the old.

Endnotes

1   Takeshi Hazama is a registered architect in Japan, although he has never been trained as an architect. He considers himself as a designer, not an architect. Hazama lived in Italy for many years, where he worked as an assistant art director for the Italian movie director Federico Fellini. He was hired by 20th Century Fox as an art director in Los Angeles for several years. He then went on to produce TV commercials in Japan. Now, he bases his business in Japan as a designer-producer. He was part of the team that came up with some of the themes for the scenes of opening and closing ceremonies of the Atlanta Olympics. Though he is a licensed architect, Hazama is what one might call a "conceptual designer." The client of the restaurant was Kiyoharu Kakazu, the former head of the Ryutou Inc., which used to be Ryukyu Seito, a local sugar manufacturing company. The site is between the city of Okinawa and the airport, and, according to

the architect, lacks good "Ki" or "quality." The tree was meant to compensate for this. It represents the gajumaru tree *(Ficus microcarpa),* which grows in the region. Hazama envisioned that that the tree would form the basis of a commercial village around it, providing "Gokujo Kokage" (the best shade under the tree). Feng-shui was also taken into consideration. Four living Gajumaru trees were placed at the bottom of the tree.

2   I would like to thank Norihiko Tsuneishi, who interviewed Hazama for me and made the necessary translations.

Credits

Photo of tree: Norihiko Tsuneishi. Image of plan reproduced with permission from Takeshi Hazama.

Dear Andrea,

Jeffrey Kipnis, in his article "Toward a New Architecture," which appeared in Architectural Design *in 1993, identifies the limitations of collage in generating a new architecture, seeing it as an exhausted tool: one that is incapable of generating a projective architecture given its reliance on recombinatorial tactics applied to existing contexts. Standing perhaps in contrast to this is R.E. Somol's very recent* [as recent as page 76] *description of a new architecture in which, by reusing and recombining (architectural) material, one creates a "surprising affect that no-one expected."*

Given your own work in this medium, and all that has occurred within architecture in the almost two decades since Kipnis's obituary of collage, is it possible to rebut Kipnis and declare collage resurrected?

—Eds.

Jeffrey Kipnis "Toward a New Architecture," *AD:*
Folding and Pliancy, Academy Editions, London, 1993
(collaged in reference to Pablo Picasso's *Bottle on a
Table*, Autumn–Winter, 1912). (For original article see
cornelljournalofarchitecture.cornell.edu)

Towards A New Architecture

Jeffrey Kipnis

Andrea Simitch

is an educator and architect. She is an associate professor at Cornell University Department of Architecture, where she has been teaching full time since 1985. She teaches courses in architectural design, architectural representation, and furniture design. She is a principal of Simitch and Warke Architects, a collaborative practice whose work includes residential, commercial, and speculative projects.

RE-Collage

The collage has generally been understood as an object, a fait accompli that exists as a record of previous operations, as a testimony to someone once having "been there" and later having "done that." Prized for its compositional values, for its associations with the heroic days of modern art, and, let's face it, as a tool for nostalgic reverie, collage has never been fully elucidated in its role as a design technique.

However, there is a clear distinction between collage as a process and collage as a thing. As an operation, collage brings into physical contact previously unrelated material, usually initiating unexpected associations and relationships. Each material brought to the collage has two responsibilities: first, to retain its own distinct color, scale, and texture, as well as the history and meanings embedded within; second, to be able to extend its characteristics to—while becoming a part of—another material. In other words, a component of collage is obliged to succumb to the whole, while retaining its own identity. This capability, whereby two previously unrelated but now adjacent materials become materially and spatially intertwined, produces a third condition, one that is constantly shifting between the original artifacts and the collective artifact that is produced. It is this constant fluctuation of the collage's spatial and material readings that can simulate the more ephemeral and fleeting characteristics of a site: characteristics that are often impossible to access.

And it is these discoveries, embedded within the processes of collage, that offer a parallel and distinct form of architectural contextualization as an alternative to the more overt forms of reiterative contextualism that have devalued the concept. Collage argues instead that the found object, the existing fragment, can participate actively in the projection of future architectures via a range of actions—material, occupational, historical, cultural, and spatial in nature—as they rub up against proposed, imported, and alternative constructions and infrastructures.

This expanded definition suggests an appropriation of multiple artifacts as active participants in any new construction; that nothing can be complete—or should ever be complete—and that a richness lies in the inevitable messiness of a collection of architectures, of textures, of programs, and of histories. And it is in this messy irresolute world that the ephemeral aspects of the building and the city are perhaps given a primary generative value for the first time, and where processes of collage can offer productive insights.

Within a collage, the impermanent and the fragmentary have the ability—the necessity even—to be appropriated by additional layers where each insists on a transformation of the fragments' latent meanings. These new layers are able to mine the various languages, references, and scales of the fragment—to give new meaning and significations to something that might have had other significant

All collages by Andrea Simitch.

legibilities prior to its coming into contact with the other, the "new." This shifti-
ness of the collage's fragments is important, as they can be simultaneously interpreted, so that concepts of contamination and borrowed meanings can exist at and
inform multiple scales. Just as Michael Graves described in his seminal article
"The Necessity for Drawing: Tangible Speculation,"[1] as the doodle moved around
the table, it was continuously reimagined and appropriated, "each mark setting up
implications for the next." But as soon as someone sketched a stair, the ability for
the drawing to remain speculative died; for it was just a plan, and at a determinate
scale.

It is these constantly shifting landscapes of multiple interpretations that have
the ability to be appropriated by multiple audiences through various lenses, a
necessity for an increasingly global audience with broad cultural references. Take,
for example, Aldo Rossi's Teatro del Mondo, constructed for the Venice Biennale
in 1979. The embedding of a floating theater within the city of Venice, by temporarily modifying the Venetian skyscape, permanently alters the way we see Venice,
as the theater's presence (both in its representations and in its realities) collects
and transforms adjacent towers into its world of extraordinary machines and
carnival structures. Rossi's tower permanently alters our perception of the existing
context—its scale, its programs, its imagined landscapes.[2]

Aldo Rossi: Teatro del Mondo © La Biennale di
Venezia—Archivio Storico delle Arti Contemporanee.
Photo: Giorgio Zucchiatti.

And while Le Corbusier's interior photographs of Villa Savoye[3] are not collages per se (though one would be dishonest not to acknowledge their explicit compositional reference to the cubist sensibilities of collage in the traditional sense), they certainly iterate the processes of collage in that they conceptually challenge and give new meaning to our perception of architectural space and sequence. Each image is carefully framed as if it is an abstracted nature morte, demanding that we understand and eventually construct movement through space not as a continuous experience but as an assemblage of lines, volumes, surfaces, and objects that together produce a collection of discreet still-lifes. These images fluctuate between deep space and shallow space, simultaneously flattening and projecting the architectural experience. Spatial events are thus represented as a series of filmic stills, superimposed and imprinted on our consciousness, initially experienced over time yet freed to be disassembled and reassembled independent of their initial spatial location.

Le Corbusier, Villa Savoye
©FLC/ARS.

Collage is not merely the grafting of previously unrostered material, as Kipnis would have us believe in *Toward a New Architecture*.[4] This indeed would demonstrate a failed attempt at heterogeneity, as it inevitably brings little blurring of boundaries, be they political, spatial, material, cultural, and so on. Here, the premise is instead that collage is not a final act but a generative and projective one, a continuously incomplete act that proposes new relationships from previously unrelated fragments. The base material no longer remains static. Not only are its edges literally destabilized by coming into close proximity with adjacent material where its colors, forms, and textures might be modified, or perhaps amplified and even recontextualized, but the contextual DNA embedded within it is instantly appropriated into new adjacent structures. Thus the material chosen, the protagonist in the act of collage, must be embedded with a critical incompleteness and willingness to be modified, a lack of absolute resistance. The material itself is a shameless accomplice in the eternal re-projection of context. Collage is neither a closed nor a final act. It is a continuously incomplete act, quite the opposite of the fixed frame and single message proposed by its consideration as a mere sum of its parts. Collage suggests that there are numerous strategies to extract the ephemeral characteristics of site: its color, its texture, its scale, its density. Every given condition is a fragment. And a "fragment" in this instance does not mean something broken or partially missing, but instead an incomplete object suggesting another body/thing or the presence of another voice/program. This concept of fragment is susceptible to multiple interpretations as it comes into proximity with alternative others. Just as Albers revealed in his color studies that a yellow color can borrow the yellow from an adjacent green, transforming it into an apparent blue, so can something like a structure's material texture be amplified or erased depending on the engagement of an adjacent structure's textural condition. It is this Bakhtinian concept of unfinalizability as a desirable perpetual state that holds the key to the creative and interactive potential of the fragment, that embedded in any fragment (utterance) is the possibility for an audience to become an accomplice. This indeterminism argues for a loss of control, for the amplification of the sensual, for an awakening to the unexpected, the found, the hidden, the neglected, and the discarded, all saturated by the potential of re-imagination. It rejects the already known, the complete, the fixed, the controlled.

For example, in Le Corbusier's 1964 Carpenter Center for the Visual Arts in Cambridge, Massachusetts, as the sidewalk is drawn into the complex, the normative condition of sidewalk to building, of urban public to institutional private becomes complicated. Suddenly, the pedestrian is thrust into the core of the building, not only blurring the boundaries of what was once more neatly defined as city versus object but transforming the pedestrian into a simultaneous actor and voyeur as he saunters between the building's volumes, both gazing into the art space and on display. Neither role is fixed, but the fluctuation between the two introduces a complex dialogue that is engaged at multiple scales.

This blurring of urban and object boundaries is perhaps more literally demonstrated in Barkow Leibinger's 2007 TRUTEC Building in Seoul. By disturbing the traditional flat plane of the glass curtain wall, it most closely constructs a literal collage by collecting its immediate context through reflections. It becomes "an urban prism where fragmented urbanscapes crystallize on the building's topographical surfaces."[5] The surface becomes an active interface between city and building, collapsing them onto one site, simultaneously projecting and anticipating.

Barkow Leibinger, TRUTEC. © Corinne Rose.

The argument here is not for a city or a building to be constructed as a collage per se—as in a superimposition of disparate elements sampled from or literally referencing a particular context. Not at all. It is simply arguing for a parallel sensibility in the making of cities and buildings; that all new structures have the responsibility to borrow, mine, amplify, and distort their meanings from their context, and that likewise, future contexts are latently embedded within these new existing structures, waiting to be mined and subsequently appropriated. This appropriation of one context into another can be observed in the horizontal cut at sitting-eye level in the southeast surface of Alvaro Siza's Church of St. Mary in Marco de Canaveses, Portugal.

Miguel Nebel, Marco de Canaveses. Photo courtesy
Miguel Nebel (http://miguelnebel2.carbonmade.com).

Through this simple act, Siza collects the distant landscape and fuses it onto the blank luminous space of the church interior, choreographing the real with the imagined, the earthly with the sacred.

Thus the (literal) collages found in these pages, for example, reveal aspects of a context that resist more conventional and singular forms of representation. These collages are all constructed out of found materials, material that is scavenged, collected, and appropriated. Here collage is understood to be a two-dimensional representational tool that indexes the more ephemeral dimensions of a subject, the more fleeting sensibilities of a context. Some operate as primary sources that reference a specific spatial or material condition, thus influencing not only the palette of collage material but also the ability of the collage to embody the textural qualities of a site. For others, color is thematically linked to context, as it is directly associated with the local inks, graphic production agencies, available paper resources, and climatic pollutions and erosions, but also as it conveys a context's unique luminous qualities as observed through the relationship between the constructed, the materials of construction, and the conditions of light. The use of text within the collage material references the various densities and grains (urban, spatial, structural, and so on) of context, just as a text's or image's scale registers a previous distance of observation. And for many collages, the actual procedures, the production methodologies that are deployed in the process of making the collage (ripping vs. cutting, layering vs. splicing, etc.) determine their spatial readings.

In Collage City, Rowe describes the collage as "a method of paying attention to the leftovers of the world ..."[6] It is these leftovers that have inspired my own work over the years: the collection of disparate objects suddenly becoming inextricably connected; the arbitrariness and inevitability of it all; the construction of new worlds that are simultaneously embedded yet distinct from where they were extracted. They resist permanence, demanding transformation into multiple worlds and interpretations. These collages are rough and slightly messy collections of worlds, worlds that are never fixed, that fluctuate spatially and materially, that carry traces of their histories while eternally projecting future narratives.

Endnotes

1 Michael Graves, "The Necessity for Drawing: Tangible Speculation," *Architectural Design*, June 1977.
2 Ibid.
3 Le Corbusier and Pierre Jeanneret, *Oeuvre Complete de 1929–1934* (Zurich: Les Editions d'Architecture Zurich, 1964), 26–27.
4 Jeffrey Kipnis, "Toward a New Architecture," *AD: Folding and Pliancy* (London: Academy Editions, 1993).
5 Ilhyun Kim, "The TRUTEC Building at Sangam Digital Media City in Extreme (ST) Seoul: A Psychogeographical Guide to Its Territorial Context," in Barkow Leibinger, *REFLECT Reflect Building in the Digital Media City Seoul, Korea* (Hatje Cantz), 40.
6 C. Rowe and F. Koetter, *Collage City* (Cambridge, MA: MIT Press, 1984), 142.

Dear Bob,

On behalf of the Cornell Journal of Architecture, *issue 8: RE, we would like to invite you to contribute an article.*

In "12 Reasons to Get Back in Shape," in Content *(p. 87) you propose an architecture that "is experienced more like a visit from an alternative world" than a "critique of this world." It is ironic to us at the* Journal *that you are undeniably R.E. and at the same time explicitly anticriticality. We would call that anti-RE. Is this Oedipal relationship with your name something that you have you have considered?*

—Eds.

Dear Editors,

Thanks for the invite. Good to know I was RE long before it became construed as critical fashion. It is not surprising to me, as you will no doubt understand, that it always seems that those with an overdeveloped sense of the ironic are most committed to the critical project.

In any case, thank you for thinking of the work, but I have to admit my now limited time for writing is aimed at exclusively projective journals (we are starting one here, entitled Flat Out*). For too long those of us on the projective side have been used as straw men for those trying to fan the flames of the critical project's dying embers. Time to move on and shift the entire context of discussion: arrivederci,* Log, Harvard Design Magazine, Grey Room, *etc. etc. Nonetheless, I am very interested in seeing the issue and the results of your labors. Hope to get up to Ithaca to see firsthand that and the rest.*

All best,
—res

RES,

Thanks for your response. We understand your position but sadly it only encourages us. Blast!

We wonder if you'd be interested in doing an interview with us at the Journal. *That way, you get it all out of your system (We'd love to hear more about shifting the context of the discussion away from criticality ... it's actually perfect, no?), but it's a really minimal time commitment on your part. It might make you feel better to think of it as a final laying to rest of this criticality stuff. One hour, that's it. What do you say?*

—Eds.

R.E. Somol

is the director of the School of Architecture at the University of Illinois, Chicago.

Being RE

In conversation with Caroline O'Donnell, and Zachary Tyler Newton, Adam Murfield, Daniel Marino, Timothy Liddell, Kyle Jenkins, Raymond Fort, Irina Chernyakova.

Caroline

As you know, for issue 8 of the *Cornell Journal of Architecture*, our theme is RE. Since you *are* R.E., I'd like to start with that: where does your name come from?

R.E.

I suppose I became R.E. in the late 80s, in my first piece of published architectural criticism, no doubt as part of the culture of postmodernism.

Caroline

In terms of that culture, you have said that Colin Rowe saw modernism as a repetition and continuity, in contrast to Peter Eisenman and Rem Koolhaas, who saw it as a break. How do *you* see the discipline?

R.E.

Breaks, but cyclical breaks. The question is whether one is more interested in suturing over those breaks and looking for continuity and lineage, or one is more interested in those moments of rupture. But the ruptures are part of that structural, cyclical game. The disciplinary question is how you approach history or tradition or precedent ...You only get to choose how to repeat, but not whether to repeat.

Caroline

Your article with Sarah Whiting, "Notes on the Doppler Effect" (2002), reads as a desire for rupture. Can you explain the context of that moment of conception?

R.E.

For me, it went back to my previous education, which was in law school, and the reason that I went to law school was to study with Roberto Unger, a social-political theorist associated with critical legal studies. Some of those people were the first to bring poststructuralist theory into legal studies: deconstructing legal texts, showing the undecidability of precedent, and so on. Law and architecture are very similar in that regard: how do you deploy precedent and swerve from it? Unger used the word *projective* to imagine new institutional relationships. This went beyond the critical Derridian model to unabashedly declare that, as with classical thought or modern social theory, there needed to be a positive theory of personality as well as a theory of politics to move forward, as opposed to simply undermining or putting quotation marks around those individual and collective formations that already exist. So for me, the projective came out of that legal, pre-architectural, engagement.

Caroline
What does the projective mean for architecture?

R.E.
I think there are three ways in which one engages audience. First, there's the normative: you produce work that confirms an existing constituency. Then there is a moment of self-consciousness where that idea of consensus breaks down, which is the birth of the critical project. In that second mode, the regime of the critical, alienation, and estrangement become the techniques to expose the fact that there is no easy consensus between form and action. The critical moment displaces an interest in the collective in order to provoke individuation. Without that moment of autonomy or separation from the world, you would still be in the world of the normative. But the question after that eruption and institutionalization of critical self-consciousness, and where I think the current urgency lies, is how to reimagine a collective again. This solicits a third way to engage audience, or the projective.

Caroline
The critical versus the projective could be aligned with the objective versus the subjective or Kant's notion of the universal subjective, which is potentially an opposition familiar to you: utopia versus heterotopia. How do you see the project in regard to this dialectic and its potential relation to notions of taste? [See page 86: "Taste Is Critical," David Salomon.]

R.E.
While the critical moment can undermine, expose, and make fun of the consensual model of modernism and its belief structure, at some point, the issue is: what next? If you are interested in forging new collectives, then at some point you have to go back to the embarrassment of that modernist possibility, but at a point at which there is no longer a convincing "true" way to represent the group, the collective. So, at that point, after the naive faith of modernism and the critical-ironic posture of postmodernism, you are in what Jeff Kipnis has called genre politics. You choose which genre you are in, and then you operate in that way. It's no longer a choice between having a true world or perpetually undermining such a faith. It's the project of appealing to different audiences to join your thing. In that sense it's a type a heterotopia or serial utopia, or nonmonogamous utopia. So the projective does recuperate some ambitions of modernism, but at the level of exaggerating in each world a degree of artifice and plasticity.

Caroline
You often use the word *cool*. What does coolness have to do with the projective?

R.E.
Whether it's associated with the modern or the contemporary, the *cool* characterizes the last moment when a certain optimism seemed possible—a precritical optimism—that is a useful complement to the projective.

Daniel

Regarding taste: I was really struck by something Jeffrey Kipnis once said to a
student. He said, If it looks like shit, it looks like shit, and I was wondering how one
could be a critic, while having the cool always embedded in one's criticism?

R.E.

The important thing is to differentiate criticism from criticality: the former can
indeed be cool and optimistic, the latter is invariably negative and pessimistic.
In the terms of McLuhan's differentiation between hot and cool media, "criticality"
(critical theory, if you will) is typically "hot" in that it requires high definition in
one channel of information: intricacy, difficulty, complexity, and so on. But the
open-endedness of the projective thrives under coolness in the sense of a degree of
vagueness and abstraction—one I have tried to associate with the concept of "shape"
and the discursive history of an antiformalist minimalism—one that solicits participation and completion due to its expedient low-definition.

Caroline

Does the rejection of the difficult in favor of the easy produce better architecture,
however one defines *better*?

R.E.

Easy is not a process, not a cause, but a desired effect. For me the easy was never
about something being easy to do, it was always about the effect of easy. We
shouldn't need to advertise our torture in public. We shouldn't need to expose the
fact that it was really hard work. Deal with it, man, it's hard work; that's your job,
now move on. What makes you good is the fact that you make hard work look easy,
not that you don't do hard work. The problem today, of course, is all those people
doing not much "work" at all, but disguising or justifying their flimsy production
under the aura of difficulty and complexity: whether in the form of writing or design.
For them, the "critical" must be maintained at all cost as the excuse for an over-
wrought complexity on autopilot.

Caroline

There's a relationship between the word *projective* and the psychological term
projection, which is about the transmission of desires onto another, and your
equating the projective with minimalism really makes sense in that it allows the
participants to project their desires onto the project. This could be the coolness you
are referring to.

R.E.

Yes, I think that it's similar to the projection onto Obama of very different agendas,
or the way in which a project like the Seattle Public Library can produce a new form
of identity for formerly disparate groups. Jesse Reiser said recently at his lecture
at UIC that he wasn't interested in contextualism like Zelig, meaning disappearing,
but actually the kind of contextualism of Chauncey Gardner, who was the vague
character everyone was able to project their desires onto. So the specific character
doesn't change, doesn't try to mimic an existing context, but the relation of the
audience is transformed by the character's ability to have different wish fulfillments

projected onto and through him.

The Seattle Public Library does that. Part of it is that you need a surprising initial image that then recalibrates the field. It needs to be imageable without representing an existing constituency, and in this way enters into a debate with Alejandro Zaera-Polo's interest in the icon. On the other extreme, you don't want to defer resemblance entirely, either, like the informalists, who mimic landscape or mimic infrastructure. You need some form of imageability, but it can't be one that represents a particular constituency, because that limits the possibility of producing crossover audiences.

Kyle

It seems like you're more promoting a plurality of voices, or the underdog, instead of any kind of system of unification.

R.E.

It's not like just any third thing will do. Part of that is how do you be a political deconstructivist. If we at least accept that there's no truth in the world, at least then we know that what everyone else is parading around as truth can't be right. Consequently, my ambition for the school, and what I think of as the goal of education, is the development of counterintuition.

Kyle

It sounds like multiple readings by a number of people is of one of the agendas or aspirations of the projective. The disciplinary knowledge that goes into the work isn't necessarily for the observer, is it?

R.E.

If you go back to Jenks's idea of multicoding, the idea is that the people will get one thing and the experts will get another; that different fragments address different constituencies, like a collage of references. I think anybody, musician, fashion designer, artist, needs to know their field inside out before they can produce those sorts of effects.

Caroline

At the end of Doppler, you say that the projective is not a capitulation to market forces, but instead it "actually respects or reorganizes multiple economies, ecologies, information systems and social groups." Does the financial crisis that was recently experienced have an effect on that, does it produce a new kind of possibility for the discipline?

R.E.

Current events certainly could be used to rescript normative agendas. Unfortunately, there has emerged a new metanarrative, loudly advertised by journalists and some of those in the field, which has to be overcome. Their new norm is that the heyday of economic excess is over, thank God, so we can roll up our sleeves and get back to work building public infrastructure. That, to me, is not a new economy; they are now just the ambulance chasers of the new (old) deal, simply confirming the current market.

Caroline

In almost every article you've written, Peter Eisenman is somehow present.
But your newer texts are—first in the Doppler and then in subsequent articles
—a strong attack on Peter's methodology. Can you explain your
ambivalence?

R.E.

It's not ambivalence. Peter established a territory for a lot of people to do things
other than what he did. That is what I'm interested in exploring. What's admirable
is that Peter is in it for the game of architecture, and he likes people to disagree
with him. The list of people he invites in to be rude to him is extensive. And that's
something you really have to give him credit for.

Also, I see—though he might not—a political dimension to what he has
done. He's precisely produced an alternative economy and ecology in architecture
that wouldn't have existed but for him. Forget the writing, forget the architecture:
he is first and foremost an institution builder. Whether it was CASE, or the Institute
of Architecture and Urban Studies, or Oppositions, or Any, he loves making groups
and publications and movements. He is a projector of institutions and a great
impresario, orchestrating and bringing together people from diverse fields and
ideologies to come and debate architecture. And you don't have to agree with
him—better if you don't.

By accident, perhaps, he always was a projective figure, he just generated it
through a formal agenda. What else is splitting the queen bed into two twin beds in
House VI, and therefore interrupting the domestic bliss, except a sadomasochistic
disciplining project of power? In other words, it comes about by a formal manipulation, but the effects are in fact behavioral, social, political, domestic. So he may
not be explicitly interested in those things, but they are in fact embedded in the
formal project. And people who overlook the effect of those forms are simply bad
critics.

Caroline

The Memorial to the Murdered Jews of Europe in Berlin is a good example, because
it's really not based on any legible reference: it's purely visceral. It produces an
experience, not a close reading.

R.E.

Yes, and I think that even he likes that aspect of it, unlike some of the more over-
heated projects. In other words, the documentary that shows the way in which
different people are enabled to do things on it illegally, how they have to police
people from sunbathing or skateboarding or whatever. There's a case where a formal
preoccupation and relentlessness releases energies and opportunities that others are
invited to complete or realize. In fact, it's very much the cool solicitation of participation one also gets in minimalism.

For me it's the stone soup phenomenon, which is the Obama and Seattle
Public Library situation: throwing an attractor into the world that starts to associate
a community around it, by virtue of being drawn to something that can encourage
that set of aftereffects.

Caroline

You and Jeff Kipnis recently commented on a dialogue between Peter and Rem in London, and the book that came out of that is called *Supercritical*. It sounds from this like the discipline is moving beyond the postcritical. Is that the case?

R.E.

You have to realize that the term *postcritical* is introduced precisely by those who would continue the critical project, by (strange as these generational bedfellows may be) the Peter Eisenmans *and* Reinhold Martins of the world. They don't want to be left behind, and so characterize their would-be adversaries as a defective, later version of themselves. Despite Martin's belated attempt to recuperate the "utopian" impulse of modernism, the point of the projective all along was to reinvigorate the power and possibility of making alternative worlds, a power that was indeed sacrificed by the critical Ph.D. factories of the east coast. Those critical doctoral centers represented the final academicization of postmodernism's ironic turn away from modernism: abdication without the humor. The projective was precisely an alternative to that subindustry of established academic architecture.

Caroline

We had Rem here last week, talking about his relationship to Ungers and Cornell [see pages 159–171], and obviously Peter has a relationship with Rowe and Cornell. These two figures, Rem and Peter, are arguably the two most important figures that we have in Architecture today and both of them have this paternal relationship with two other important figures here. Is it that resistance that produced what they are today? Is resistance necessary?

R.E.

It's not a question of resistance, because it's not a choice. To operate at the highest levels of a cultural discipline, you have to work with the material and discourses at hand, and figure a way to redirect them, to cheat them out of becoming historical facts. This is Harold Bloom's anxiety of influence—which is that to establish yourself you have to establish your predecessors. Every strong poet is first a strong critic, and needs to produce a misreading of a previous poet. I think that's what both Rem and Peter do brilliantly. But resistance implies a critical form of repetition, and therefore is a limited case, and not so useful in discussing how Peter or Rem operate today.

Caroline

You hold up Rem as somebody whose work is potentially projective. But then Peter, in *Ten Canonical Buildings* chooses Jussieu Library and relates it to Le Corbusier's Palais des Congrès project for Strasbourg. How can Rem be your figurehead while exhibiting this referentiality?

R.E.

I don't think that rearranging genetic material for new ends precludes the projective. Even the paranoid-critical method as Rem defines it: we only have a deck of cards, we don't like how they got played out, so all we can do is reshuffle the evidence. And I think that is what he is doing. He's reshuffling the deck of cards he's been given to produce new effects. No one is obsessed with originality and it's neither necessary nor desired for the projective. So really you are saying, "If I put these things together, I will have a surprising affect that people didn't expect before"— it's not that the material isn't getting reused. And so I think the question is: is it getting reused in ways that people already know? Which, in the case of the Corb repetition, is Richard Meier. If you look at a Richard Meier house, you know that it's Corbusier on steroids. If you look to Villa Dall'Ava, there's a vague resemblance to certain aspects of Corbusianism and the five points but they are exerted into a different domain.

Kyle

Isn't this idea of projective heterotopias at odds with the reshuffling of the cards that you are dealt? You're very consciously pulling things which are very recognizable and mashing them together in a way which makes them unique and new, which seems different from, but somehow wed with what you're discussing.

R.E.

I think your job as a critic is to be a cool hunter in that way. And in a sense find material in the world and rearrange it. My secret project is the Johnson Museum by I.M. Pei on this campus. I love that thing. Part of the reason why I love it is that Klaus Herdig, a student of this school, hates it. For him, it's all that's wrong with architecture as the "decorated diagram," but my positive call for the cartoon plan is just another way to say decorated diagram: cartoon instead of decoration, plan instead of diagram. And I love all the projects that Herdig says are bad. Systematically you can read that book as a monograph on cartoon style: the totemic diagrams, or the concretized diagrams, and so on. His "proper" Roweian formalism couldn't allow him to appreciate that project. But it's also true that the Pei project can't be appreciated without Neutelings Riedijk and a series of contemporary projects that allow you then to see it as a false origin for that genealogy.

Caroline

Now that you are the director at UIC, you finally have the chance to teach the projective. But it seems like it's a lot easier to teach the critical because it's referential. It seems like the critical becomes easy when it's taught whereas the projective becomes less easy. So how do you teach that? Or, as you have put it in the past: How do you teach green dots?

R.E.

The first year I was there we radically restructured the curriculum, and for the first year just basically appropriated Alejandro Zaera Polo's alternatives of control and power and decided that the Fall studio would be about control—the internal geometric protocols—and the Spring would be about power. And so, sotto voce, the two studios are the Eisenman studio and the Koolhaas studio, to get those pedagogies and legacies out right away in the first year and basically start the contemporary discipline from there, from that conversation. It's the same way that Rowe and Slutzky and Hejduk started from the Domino and the van Doesburg. Their idea was that modern architecture is space and structure. There is also truth in what Colin Rowe once said: What you teach in the first year is what you want them to rebel against in their last year. So for me, I think that you need a firm critical foundation in order to end up with a projective education. I think you need to know the nuts and bolts of your discipline, which is not the same as the nuts and bolts of construction.

Caroline
Does the issue of sustainability fit into your thesis?

R.E.
Sustainability is no thesis. It's the new panacea for having no thesis. This is the lecture that I've been giving over that past year, which discusses the difference between "-ities" and "-isms." I'm on the side of -isms and not -ities. And so all of the -ities, I can do without, because for me they are not disciplinary issues. So affordability, sustainability, interdisciplinarity, everything that ends in -ity or -ability is out of the question because it's a kind of LEED check-off. And once you're in the world of averaging out check-offs, you've left the world of ideological projection, and therefore a cultural field, which is what I maintain architecture is.

Caroline
Fair enough, I agree with you. But I want to disagree with you on something you said recently in a lecture at Otis College of Art and Design. [See excerpts of this lecture at http://www.youtube.com/watch?v=QVnElp-Qgdw.] It was a quote from Martin Scorsese's *Departed*, when Jack Nicholson says, "I don't want to be a product of my environment, I want my environment to be a product of me." I don't think it necessarily follows that being a product of one's environment is a bad thing. There are examples in nature where being a product of your environment is really a good thing. The giraffe, in terms of genetic evolution, is a product of its environment. With its food source at the top of the trees, evolutionary survival depended on the elongation of the neck, plus re-adjustments to heart and ankles to allow for groundwater drinking. The giraffe's map of the world might consist of just treetops and watering holes. It's a product of its own particular environmental analysis. If architecture was fundamentally reactive in this way, it could potentially have a sustainable consequence. What's wrong with architecture being the consequence of its environment?

R.E.
Well, clearly it's not very projective in the sense of installing artificial worlds into the world. And in fact, for me, my problem with the -ities, sustainability among them, is that it's no different than indexicality or parametrics, which to me is just how do you accommodate the forces in the world as they exist? You don't try to reimagine a world, you just say these are the forces that we are stuck with. And so there's a kind of essentialism or necessitarianism that I object to.

Zachary
I'm interested in the paradox of being a "projective critic." Is there the potential as a critic to be projective?

R.E.

I am nostalgic for the era of the generalist, and the people who wore many hats, and I think that Peter and Rem are two exemplars of that moment where it wasn't a case of the critic-historian versus the architect. They would do both jobs and jump back and forth. That's still a territory that I want to occupy. It's a territory that has shrunk in recent years.

In the context of a collaborative practice, I have produced built work. It's probably minor work in the constellation of the world. It was important for me to do and was an attempt (with a self-imposed budget and an idiot for a client) to combine these issues of modernism and mass culture, which is what I was interested in. How do you hybridize that model as an alternative to the way that New Urbanism hybridized the vernacular and the Classical as a potential thing in the world that you could proliferate? That was the question. Of course, I also simply wanted a pool.

I don't see any medium of architecture as privileged over any other. So, to me, a book and a building—one is not higher in the hierarchy of architectural possibility. There are media in the world: buildings, writing, painting, films ... and then there's architecture. And architecture transects those horizontally. So part of architecture is the world of building, but not all of it. Part of architecture is the world of writing, but not all of it. To be a projective architect doesn't mean one of these media, it actually means deploying the many media at your disposal.

Zachary

You have spoken of a nostalgia for print, and an ambivalence for, or even a dislike for the blogosphere, but it seems that since that's where the dialogue and conversation is moving, that's something that definitely needs to be engaged with. How do you gather a community there in the projective model?

R.E.

My problem with the blogosphere is the fact that it becomes amateur hour, and so disciplinary knowledge evaporates when it becomes a more or less a thumbs-up thumbs-down solicitation of peoples' thoughts on something, with good results being how many people liked a person's work. That's the downside of participation. But to me it's the mirror of Mark Wigley saying that architects write about their own work, so we shouldn't or don't have to. That attitude abdicates the role of contemporary criticism in favor of specialist scholarship. The blogosphere and the tenurable Ph.D. are mirror sides of the same phenomenon, which is eliminating the generalist from the field in place of expert criticism or a public audience.

Daniel

Is that the ugly face of the cool? That quick response, that informality, "uneditedness."

R.E.

There might be a sort of McLuhan response here; he says that all cool media eventually become hot. So there is a way in which that form of demagogic, "bottom-up" vote becomes a new form of hot media. I think it's a failure of critics to model an alternative position to their presumed "real-time" audience.

Caroline

In *Pidgin* 1, you are quoted as declaring that nobody reads anymore. How does our not reading affect the production of architecture? If we take seriously that nobody reads anymore, that means that nobody is going to read this interview. So now that nobody is listening, what do you want to say?

R.E.

To the extent architecture is a cultural discipline, its task is to propose artificial worlds. Thus, despite the current calls for architecture to become a new form of civil engineering, I tend to think that architecture is more like fashion. When Jesse Reiser and Stan Allen invented infrastructuralism in the early 90s, alongside the digital, paperless studios of the same moment, it was an -ism. Today, because of an external shift in the market and public policy, architecture has dropped the -ism and now infrastructure has become just another fact in a new era of necessitarian politics. All I want to say is, don't ever mistake your cultural practice for a set of facts. Once you do, you will have absolutely no leverage in the world that our discipline seems so desperate to engage.

David Salomon

with Paul Andersen, is the author of the book The Architecture of
Patterns. *He currently teaches architectural theory at Cornell University
Department of Architecture and the University of Pennsylvania.*

Taste Is Critical

> *... taste governs every free—as opposed to rote—human response. Nothing is
> more decisive.*
>
> Susan Sontag

Long associated with subjectivity, frivolity, and pleasure, taste is notorious for
being difficult to generalize. It is, we have been told, the antithesis of reason and the
critical. However, in revisiting theories of taste—in particular those put forward by
David Hume and Susan Sontag—one recognizes that it is both false and dangerous
to have to choose between taste and these other modes of thought. This is especially
true for aesthetic practices such as architecture. Instead, the relationship between
these categories can be better understood as complementary, not contradictory.

In every dictionary definition of *critical* the operative term is *judgment,* specifically, judgments that are accurate, precise, and decisive; are negative or "censo-
rious," and are skillful with regard to literary or artistic works. Something that is
critical is *pro*scriptive: providing advice for what *not to do* aesthetically. In terms of
architectural discourse and production, these definitions beg three questions: First,
what skills and knowledge are required in order to be critical? Second, could one
simultaneously be critical and *pre*scriptive? And last, is taste the key to answering
both of these questions?

The philosopher David Hume described *taste* using concepts and terms that are
surprisingly similar to those used to describe *critical.* For him, taste is the faculty
employed for making judgments, specifically those regarding sensorial and aesthetic
phenomenon. Taste is a form of intelligence; a way of knowing the world by recon-
ciling sensorial experience with cognition via one's imagination; a faculty whose
function is to establish connections between seemingly unlike categories, spaces,
temporalities, and so on. It is the flip side of the critical: criticism dealing with
negative assessment and feedback, taste concerning those associated with positive
judgments and feedback.

In his essay, "Of the Standard of Taste,"[1] Hume notes that most "common
sense" notions of taste maintain that all "sentiments" are equally true because they
cannot be linked to a concept outside of themselves. In this conception, everybody's
individual taste is "right." This is opposed to judgments of "understanding" (as
found in philosophy and science), which are grounded by their adherence to external
referents and are "always conformable to that standard."

However, this lack of a unique standard does not render aesthetic experiences
inconsequential or relative. Nor does it mean that sentiment and understanding are
mutually exclusive modes of thought. While there may be no external or a priori
rules governing the production and reception of aesthetic phenomenon, Hume argues
that they are grounded, like all practical knowledge, "on experience and on the observation of the common sentiments of human nature." In this realm, the works that

are deemed the best are those that have withstood the test of time, and are generally agreed to exhibit the highest qualities of the art. This emphasis on historical continuity, he argues, accounts for why the rhetorical style of Cicero is still held in high regard even after the ideas that informed it have been rendered obsolete.

Still, who is allowed to establish and enforce this canon? What skills and qualities must the critic have to enable her to recognize the affinity between "form and sentiment" in works that either continue to earn praise or new ones that do? For Hume, people who can recognize otherwise hidden qualities and who are able to discriminate between better and worse examples are those who have taste. For him, the characteristics of and criteria for this capacity are: a delicacy of imagination; good sense (i.e., reason); the regular practice of these skills; constant comparisons between examples; a lack of prejudiced thinking.[2]

While he makes it clear that delicacy is a gift of birth, it, along with the others factors, can be improved or diminished over time depending on how often and well it is exercised and experienced. He also makes it clear that while the principles underlying this faculty are consistent, the specific skills and qualities necessary for developing one's taste are historically conditioned, differ over time, from place to place, and from one discursive field to the next. The principles and practices of taste may not change, yet objects and contexts in which they emerge do. One must not only learn how to use taste, but one must do so within the confines of a specific cultural, historical, and aesthetic context. This requires one to fine-tune one's faculties in order to determine when something is still relevant or superior and when something new is worthy of entering the canon.

But, does not the establishment of a canon, via expertise, knowledge, taste, or otherwise, preclude or at least slow down diversity and innovation? Late in his essay, Hume notes that there are conditions which, although not enough to undermine "all boundaries of beauty and deformity," can account for and accept difference within the established order. The internal and external conditions that produce this variety being: the "different humours in men" and the "particular manners and opinions of our age and country."[3]

How then is this not a return to there being multiple, if not an infinite number of "right" sentiments? Hume's answer is that while there are not countless modes of aesthetic production, there is a plurality of them, each of them governed by their own standards. He takes pains not to establish a hierarchy among these different genres or sensibilities. The sublime, the tender, and raillery are equally valid. While it is difficult if not impossible to employ the principles of taste from one medium to the next, within each medium—or from one era to another—one can be quite critical of the varying degrees of quality. Taste is thus neither universal nor infinitely fragmented. It is plural, yet specific with regard to history and medium. This tolerance of multiple modes is the opposite of the prejudice that prevents one from developing one's taste. Having a specific sensibility or preference for one thing does not mean negating other equally valid ones. It would be a mistake, Hume notes, for "a critic to confine his approbation to one species or style of writing, and condemn all the rest."[4] He continues, the selection of our preferred sensibilities occurs in the same way that we chose our friends, picking ones with whom we share the same "humour and disposition." Taste is the faculty of recognition, camaraderie, and empathy. Empirically, via trial and error and habit, taste produces collective sensibilities from the aggregation of individual positions. It is political in that no position is universally recognized as valid, therefore, it must be defended and/or redefined in order for it to remain effective and relevant.

Moving On

> *... Intellectual progress usually occurs through sheer abandonment of questions together with both of the alternatives they assume—an abandonment that results from their decreasing vitality and a change of urgent interest. We don't solve them: we get over them.*
>
> John Dewey

What is essential for Hume, regardless of sensibility, time period, or culture, is that "morality" not be undermined or obfuscated. Sentiment and good taste cannot trump immoral acts. Good form cannot justify bad behavior.

Such is the accusation against what Robert E. Somol and Sarah Whiting call the "projective" in architectural discourse and production. To its detractors, the projective is dangerous because (1) it abandons both the means and the ends of "the critical" project; (2) it replaces them either with the facile charms of pragmatics and decoration, and (3) it furthers the agenda of the social, economic, and aesthetic status quo by failing to provide truly oppositional (i.e., structural or utopian) alternatives to it.[5]

While it is true that the negative, proscriptive logic of the critical have been challenged by the projective, and new modes of production have been proposed, it does not necessarily follow that this is a sign of capitulation to the forces that be. In fact, it would seem to be the opposite. Projective architects' adaptation of ornamental, banal, and graphic sensibilities echoes Hume's recognition of the need for the "particular manners and opinions of [an] age" to be developed in order for them to relate to a contemporary audience and problem.

Similarly, the emphasis on the plural is an important tenet of the projective, and represents an epistemological shift from the establishment of logical "if-then" statements, to the posing of aesthetic "What if...?" questions. This emphasis on multiple alternatives is not to be confused with utopian solutions, which seek to carve out a space of resistance or negation. Rather, it is a call for the proliferation of virtual alternatives that do not yet exist within current conditions.

Despite these divisions, there are some moments of continuity between the projective and the critical. An important example being Somol and Whiting's emphasis on disciplinarity or autonomy, which they maintain, following K. Michael Hayes, is paradoxically understood as a *precondition* for engagement with the social, not a retreat from it.[6] The concept of autonomy is, of course, a touchstone of one of the founders of critical theory, Theodore Adorno, who argued that the critical work of art is at once generated by conditions found in the world, yet is simultaneously separate or isolated from it.

This paradoxical condition serves as a reminder of those ideas and actions that are impossible at any one historical moment, and thus have no home in the world other than in the estranged world of artistic form. Such forms are not intended to produce pleasure or pain; rather, they at once reveal and position themselves between human beings and the conditions that oppress them *now*. It is a temporal state that has been made formal.[7] Such aesthetic objects or forms are less uncanny (at once familiar and strange) but untimely; they are simultaneously early and late, or old and new.

What Somol and Whiting find objectionable is that by 2002 this previously exceptional position of critical architecture—straddling culture and form, engagement and estrangement—was deemed the de facto position attributed to all legitimate forms of architectural production. Further, there was seemingly only one long-standing aesthetic technique for articulating this position: *indexicality*. In addition to it being a representational rather than a propositional mode of production, the continued focus of critical architecture on a particular tactic runs counter to Adorno's position that critical aesthetic strategies (and by extension, forms) needed to evolve in order to effectively address contemporary conditions; this capacity to adapt being a key characteristic of the avant-garde he championed.

Both the relevance and historically specific status of the form of the autonomous art object suggest that the necessary skill for designers and critics alike is to recognize when the context has changed significantly enough to warrant the devising of new strategies (formal and otherwise) for operating effectively in it. For the projective, this means that not only must one demonstrate what is missing in the world, but one must attempt to create new aesthetic and social formations by directly engaging the hegemonic tactics, techniques, and forms active in contemporary society. In this sense, the critique of the critical is less a question of substance than style. The dissatisfaction with and desire to show what can and cannot be found in contemporary society remains consistent, but the forms, and the level of engagement, have changed in order for them to be untimely in a different and more active way. This can be seen, for example, in the willingness to engage site and market mechanisms—such as design guidelines and marketing strategies—in order to more directly place oneself within the means of production, rather than stand aside from them.

However, when architecture engages these arenas, its legitimacy and effectiveness still rests on its ability to generate and design forms and sensibilities that are likewise untimely. It is this ability that allows architecture, when it engages issues outside its traditional scope—Somol and Whiting cite "economics and civic politics"—to do so not as experts in these subjects, nor as critics (i.e., negative assessors) of them, but as "experts in how design can [actively] affect these fields."[8] Though Somol and Whiting do not explicitly define the term *design,* it is clear that it is not meant as a method of solving problems that have more than one right answer (as proposed by Herbert Simon). Rather, the understanding of design here seems closer to the creation of objects and events via aesthetic means. Following Hume then, this suggests that in order to be effective, architectural design, theory, and criticism must not only be armed with good intentions and knowledge, but with taste.

New Sensibilities

One of the most astute accounts regarding the social and cultural importance of creating new sensibilities and expanded tastes, and the need to breed more of them, is found in Susan Sontag's essay "Notes on Camp." Among the qualities

Sontag found valuable about camp was the fact that it wasn't conceived of as an exchange of bad for good art, or low for high taste. Rather, it rejected such false choices, instead offering "for art (and life) a different—*a supplementary*—set of standards" to make and judge cultural production.[9] Specifically, camp was understood as a contrasting addition to the "classical, serious, accurate and high minded" taste, and to the then more contemporary sensibility of "seriousness, anguish, cruelty, derangement" that described much modern art. If the former emphasized beauty, harmony, and completeness, and the latter violence and fragmentation, camp was an aesthetic of frivolity and openness, "incarnate[ing] a victory of 'style' over 'content.'"[10]

This emphasis on style is not to be misunderstood as a narcissistic retreat into the pleasure of form for form's sake. As Gregory Bateson argued a few years later, the types of messages that are sent and received via aesthetic means are different than those conveyed via "content" or reason. Form not only communicates differently, it communicates categorically different kinds of messages, ones that cannot be sent via linear cognitive processes. Bateson was fond of quoting Isadora Duncan's comment: "If I could say it, I wouldn't have to dance it" to make his point.[11] For Bateson, the message aesthetic phenomenon sent was about "patterns that connect," at a subconscious level, all living and thinking "minds" with one another. The production and recognition of aesthetic encounters, however, was not limited to the fine arts or to certain aspects of nature. Rather, it could be found in a plethora of places and processes. In fact, for Bateson, the use of subconscious or primary processes necessary to both make and experience art was an important antidote to contemporary society's emphasis on purposeful, rational, linear, and conscious processes. Not because they were inherently liberating or resistant, but because it made one have to literally think differently (subconsciously, habitually), requiring one to find connections, or patterns, that linked disparate cultural and natural phenomenon.[12]

Sontag shares Bateson's expanded, formal, epistemological, and political notion of aesthetic creation and reception. For her, camp had serious ethical implications, as it revealed "another kind of truth about the human situation, another experience of what it is to be human—in short, another valid sensibility";[13] a sensibility that, not unimportantly, was often produced and championed by a marginalized social group: (a subset of) urban gay men. Camp, like all sensibilities, became an avenue for generating and legitimizing a different form of personal and collective identity. Despite appearances, camp was neither im- nor amoral, nor anti-intellectual. Sontag notes that while morals are essential and generative, they are also somewhat fixed. What really counts, she argues, is "the style in which ideas are held. The ideas about morality and politics ... [in camp are] held in a special playful way,"[14] a way that makes them valuable to someone who can discern the characteristics of this sensibility, that is, someone with a taste for camp. In this case camp, as a sensibility that may initially have appeared foreign, crude, and superficial, can, with practice, constant comparison, and good sense, become an ever more delicate and better-understood way of knowing the world.

Critical Taste

Historically, camp emerged and was effective when a culture, or a part of a culture "realize[d] that 'sincerity' is not enough"[15] to create social change. The then current (circa 1964) sensibility of seriousness was deficient because it was neither able to distance itself from reality nor was it recognized as directly engaging itself within current ideological battles. By introducing a new standard—"artifice as an ideal"—camp proposed an untimely interjection into an era (the cold war) that was serious to the point of suicide.

Nearly half a century later, we find ourselves in a similarly serious moment. Thus, it is not too surprising that an architecture that emphasizes the quirky, the humorous, and the campy has emerged. For firms like OMA, Herzog & de Meuron, Bjake Ingles Group (BIG), Jurgen Meyer H., Atelier Bow Wow, and SANAA, humor is clearly an important goal of the work. While they may stress this effect over a project's meaning, structure, or performance, these requirements are far from ignored. In fact, these practices are hyperdisciplinary in their attention on the manipulation of spaces, surfaces, shapes, and activities. However, these are initially developed and distributed according to a sensibility, as opposed to starting with efficiency or some other seemingly more expedient logic.

One tactic that is often taken up by these firms to produce a project's sensibility is *patterning;* patterns that can best be described as explicit and vivid.[16] These two qualities are often combined to produce work that is simultaneously clear and complex; both blunt and extravagant. The result is work that has the qualities of immediacy and intensity; effects that don't wear off and that penetrate beyond the surfaces into the inner workings of both buildings and minds.

Perspective, Ciudad del Flamenco, City of Jerez de la Frontera, Spain, 2003–2007, Herzog & de Meuron, © Herzog & de Meuron.

Vividness is a quality often found in the work of Herzog & de Meuron. In their design for the Ciudad de Flamenco (Jerez de la Frontera, Spain, 2003), a two-dimensional pattern inspired by Gypsy culture, Arabic iconography, and 20th-century graffiti establishes a rough yet lyrical sensibility that literally permeates the tectonics of the project. By rescaling, repeating, and thickening the pattern, they are able to transform it into a malleable and permeable perimeter wall that seamlessly morphs as it takes on the various roles of low building wall, courtyard fence, and structural skin for the museum tower. This surprisingly robust pattern maintains its intricate feel even as it adjusts itself to the more strict logics of a construction system. Despite these multiple transformations and performances, the edgy graphic quality of the original is consistently present. As a result, the building addresses an unusual architectural question: What if we make a building out of ornament/graffiti?

Detail of Wall Pattern, Ciudad del Flamenco, City of Jerez de la Frontera, Spain, 2003–2007, Herzog & de Meuron, © Herzog & de Meuron.

Abstraction of Arabic Calligraphy

Rotation and Superimposition

Simplification and Extraction

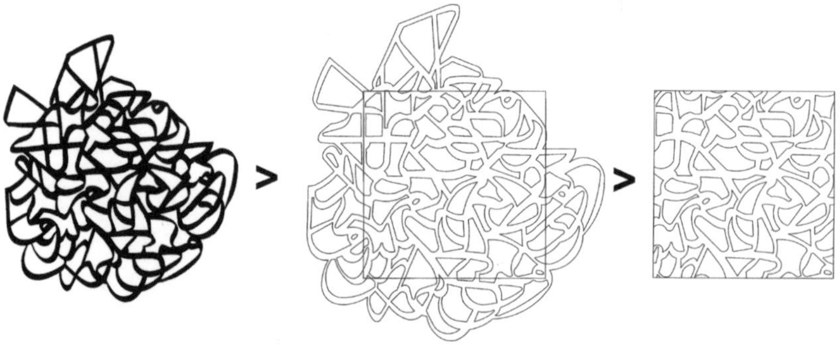

In BIG's Holbaek Kasba housing project (Holbaek, Denmark, 2006), the process is presented as if it were an exercise in pattern making. The diagrams illustrating the project depict how an orthogonal grid gave way to skewed pentagon shaped forms and a hexagonal pattern of streets. The multicolored plans and axons of the units (which are themselves highly differentiated) extend the explicit quality of the drawings. In comparison, the predominately white model is relatively subdued, despite housing an unexpected variety of unit types. And yet the clarity, intensity, and campy quality of the drawings is matched by the model's graphic depiction of the alternately white and green street surfaces and the deep shadows cast into them. In short, every depiction reaffirms the explicit quality one expects from an ideogram, an effect one hopes the built version would also contain.

Plan and Section Diagrams, Unit Plans, and Model, Holbaek Kasba, Holbaeck, Denmark, Bjarke Ingles Group 2006. Images courtesy of Bjarke Ingles Group.

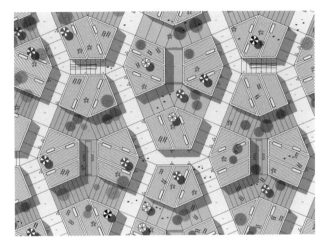

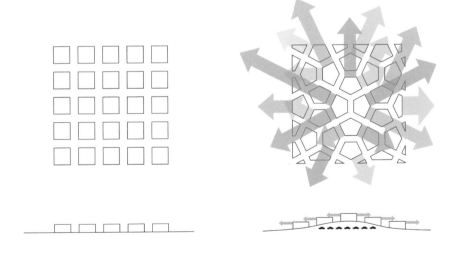

In contrast to these more unexpected sources and solutions, SANAA's commitment to reanimating the white box has resulted in no less explicit or vivid pattern. Theirs is a quiet yet intense patterning. This paradox is evident in their drawings, which despite the paucity of ink, are forceful in their simplicity. The plans and sections of the Zollverein School of Management (Essen, Germany, 2006) are so lacking in expression that they threaten to raise banality to new heights. The elevations and facades are slightly more revealing but are still subdued; the apertures bunching around two out of the four corners producing the most intense image of the exterior. It is only with the model, and finally the building itself, where more conventionally expressive qualities are exposed. In what otherwise would be described as rough, unfinished, warehouse-like spaces, the interiors are enlivened, even haunted, by the strangely scaled patterns produced by the shadows produced on these unadorned concrete surfaces.

As these distorted, fleeting, and hard to account for rectangular and square outlines spill across the floors and up the walls, they generate an unexpectedly distorted and strange patterns; ones that intensify the simple, enigmatic, yet lighthearted quality of the project. While every building with apertures might produce this generic effect, it is the intensity and directness with which SANAA manipulates this architectural inevitability that enables them to generate a different sensibility, one that is at once understated, explicit, and vivid. This project, and their work in general, asks: How can one create unique ends using the most conventional of means?

Zollverein School of Management and Design, Essen, Germany. Plan (Ground to 3rd floor), Elevation, Exterior, and Interior. Courtesy of SANAA. 2006. Photographs © thomasmayerarchive.com.

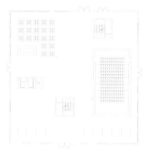   

That many contemporary architectural artifacts, have camplike qualities should not be understood as another postmodern quotation. Rather, this "work on form" echoes Bateson's interest in the epistemological instrumentality of form. For Bateson, an aesthetic object's effectiveness relies not on its meaning, or on its capacity to perform a specific task. Rather, it must act sensorially (e.g., make you smile or laugh), which in turn produces a feeling of "recognition and empathy" between oneself, the work, and the larger context in which the encounter occurs.[17] The production and recognition of such affects is dependent on the presence of taste in both the design and its reviewer. However, not everyone will be able to immediately recognize, or empathize with, every sensibility. That capacity, Bateson argues, requires both producers and consumers of aesthetic phenomena (which are broadly defined to include many categories of objects and events) to hone their skills of making and judging.[18] That is, they must exercise and improve their taste.

Today's explicit and vivid patterns require new modes of criticism to effectively examine, develop, and make judgments about the effects they produce. It requires that we simultaneously expand and refine our criticism and our taste— as Sontag did in her "Notes"—in order to see what new architectural and social effects and constituencies they can attract, produce, or inhibit. To start, such criticism requires making careful and repeated aesthetic observations and comparisons. It also demands making judgments that are not prejudiced but remain political; that is, far from producing consensus, they enable one to effectively choose sides. And yet, what does such work oppose? How does focusing on seemingly autonomous disciplinary issues—walls, windows, streets, and surfaces, as well as plans, sections, and elevations—make architectural discourse and production critical and/or political? Who or what does it emancipate? For starters, the discipline. As with the camp, explicit and vivid patterns and sensibilities can help to loosen the tyranny from the all-too-few modes of production and expression currently available to architecture. While it does not, and cannot, offer a specific alternative to institutional power, it does what aesthetic practices do best: challenge that power's sensibility by proposing alternative ones. In other words, taste is something that architecture must be critical with, not of.

Endnotes

1 David Hume, "Of the Standard of Taste," in *Aesthetics: A Comprehensive Anthology,* Steven M. Cahn and Aaron Meskin (eds.) (Malden, MA: Blackwell, 2008), 103–112.
2 Ibid.
3 Ibid.
4 Ibid.
5 George Baird, "'Criticality' and Its Discontents," *Harvard Design Magazine* 21 (Fall 2004/Winter 2005); Reinhold Martin, "Critical of What?" *Harvard Design Magazine* 22 (Spring/Summer 2005).
6 Robert Somol and Sarah Whiting, "Notes Around the Doppler Effect and Other Moods of Modernism," *Perspecta* 33 (2002): 72–77.
7 Theodor Adorno, from "Aesthetic Theory," in *Aesthetics: A Comprehensive Anthology*, Steven M. Cahn and Aaron Meskin (eds.) (Malden, MA: Blackwell, 2008), 358–369. In Adorno's words "unresolved antagonisms of reality reappear in art in the guise of immanent problems of artistic form"; form which presents both "an aesthetically complete object, while preserving within it the traces or fracture of those elements which resisted integration" and thus remain estranged, or absent from it, such as political and economic reform.
8 Somol & Whiting, op cit.
9 Susan Sontag, "Notes on Camp," in *Against Interpretation and Other Essays* (New York: Farrar, Straus & Giroux, 1966), 286.
10 Ibid., 287–288.
11 Gregory Bateson, "Style, Grace and Information in Primitive Art," *Steps to an Ecology of Mind* (New York: Ballantine, 1972), 137–138.
12 Ibid., 144–147.
13 Sontag, 287.
14 Ibid., 288.
15 Ibid.

16 On patterns, see Paul Andersen and David Salomon, *The Architecture of Patterns* (New York: Norton, 2010); and Andersen and Salomon, "Promiscuous Patterns, Synthetic Architecture," *Harvard Design Magazine* 31 (Fall/Winter 2009–2010).

17 Gregory Bateson, *Mind and Nature: A Necessary Unity* (New York: Dutton, 1979), 8.

18 Bateson, 147–149.

Philip Johnson & Sibyl Moholy-Nagy

Philip Cortelyou Johnson was an influential figure in the architecture discipline in the 20th century. Most notable works include his private residence, the Glass House, the Abby Aldrich Rockefeller Sculpture Garden at the Museum of Modern Art, the AT&T Building, and the New York State Theater at Lincoln Center. He was awarded the first Pritzker Architecture Prize for his seminal contributions to the architecture, art, and design of the 20th century.

Sibyl Moholy-Nagy was an architectural and art historian. She taught visual education, architectural history, and the history of art, with a final appointment at Pratt Institute as a professor of history and theory of architecture. She was a contributing editor to Progressive Architecture, *the* Architectural Forum, Perspecta, *and other architectural journals.*

Unsolicit**ed Comments

In *Mart Stam's Trousers,* Dolf Broekhuizen presents a touching set of correspondences between Philip Johnson and J.J.P. Oud during the Second World War titled "Mr. Oud Loses Ornament—Correspondence between Philip Johnson and J.J.P. Oud, 1931–55." The content meanders between architectural criticism and expressions of need and gratitude for help during years of paucity in the Netherlands. The correspondence reveals, Broekhuizen notes, that "the genealogy of modern architecture was determined to a significant extent by individual quests, opinion, doubts, and friendships."

In researching these multifaceted letters as part of our investigations in criticism and correspondence for issue 8: RE, the editors discovered the following correspondence that is yet another captivating interweaving of personal warmth and precise criticism; a narrative of two individuals who care deeply about the practice and criticism of architecture, as well as about each other.

The letters refer to two articles, one by each correspondent, the first page of each being presented here. For the full article, see the *Cornell Journal of Architecture* website, cornelljournalofarchitecture.cornell.edu.

—Eds.

By Philip Johnson

Is Sullivan the father of functionalism?

The Chicago master who has become a myth is

re-evaluated on the centenary of his

birth by a distinguished modern architect

The reactions that follow were inspired by the recent spate of publicity on the centenary of Sullivan's birth. The exhibition at the Chicago Art Institute, directed by Edgar Kaufmann, and the book by John Szarkowski (University of Minnesota Press) whose photographs form the basis of that exhibition, were the chief events of the autumn. The book (unfortunately I could not visit the exhibition), is full of beautiful photographs of Sullivan's work, but much has been omitted (where are the Ryerson and the Wainwright tombs, both better than the Getty, which is included?) and much else is photographed anew which might better be left unphotographed. The Carson, Pirie and Scott Building and the Schiller Theater, defaced in recent years, exist in old photographs which are far better than the author's. The Guaranty Building, however, gets the full treatment and we are grateful. Sullivan lovers, however, should watch for a volume announced by the Horizon Press for next year; it promises to be the first definite publication of the complete works of Adler and Sullivan.

It is twenty-four years since I first made a Sullivan pilgrimage to Chicago to wonder at the Gage Building façade, the Auditorium Building and Carson, Pirie and Scott. Today, after almost a generation, what of his reputation? I am not scholarly enough to evaluate anew the work of one of America's great artists, but writing only as one of the architects under his influence and aroused by the present furor on the centenary of his birth, I want to examine his work once more.

I find I am by no means as sure as I was then. Apart from the Wainwright Building in St. Louis and the Guaranty Building in Buffalo, do I feel in myself any genuine respect for his work? Can I sense any influence? Quite honestly, no.

To me, the Sullivan story reads somewhat differently from the current encomiums. Here was a young Richardsonian designer, full of talent, who had a gift for Whitman-like prose that transformed the merest platitude of tautology into an aphorism. He was the second best Richardsonian architect in the city in the great period of Chicago architecture. (John Root was the best.) As designer of tall buildings, he was (for a while and for only two buildings) great. But even in these two buildings the designs are all Richardson, i.e. in masonry terms, in contradistinction to the Reliance Building of Burn-

Father of the skyscraper?

"John Root was the best" follower of architect Richardson, not Sullivan, as is so widely believed. The undecorated beauty of the Monadnock Block which Burnham and Root built in Chicago, 1889, is "pure masonry and pure form."

ham and Root [p. 45] designed in terms of steel, which in the '90's was the emerging structural system.

We cannot today think of Sullivan as the "first to form fitting clothing for tall buildings." Perhaps the undecorated beauty of the Monadnock Block [p. 44] does not count in the tally of skyscrapers since it was pure masonry, pure form. Perhaps the Reliance Building, on the other hand, is no beauty; but it pointed the way more clearly to the future than did Sullivan's work.

After the Wainwright and Guaranty Buildings of the mid 90's, nothing Sullivan did ever could be called anything but second rate. The ornament, which was always Sullivan's first love rather than structure or massing, became painfully ugly and the fenestration more and more arbitrary and ill-proportioned. He seemed not to have become aware of Wright's great revolution of 1900 in architectural form. Wright's "breaking of the box," which became the basis of all thinking in modern architecture, Sullivan never noticed. He remained a man of the "pencil" in his designs and a Richardsonian in his building.

History has been kind to Louis Sullivan. The alcholism, the sex troubles, his rejection by the public before he was fifty, the lonely death are all grist to the romantics' mill. In addition, being exiled in a sense from architecture by 1904, he had twenty years of life in which to write his apologia. Like Napoleon at St. Helena, he created his own myth while he was alive, but

The Reliance Building, Chicago [left], 1895, by Burnham and Root, in its use of steel, pointed the way to the future more clearly than Sullivan ever did; and the now-unfashionable McKim's Boston Public Library, built in 1887, has "far purer" design than most of Sullivan's anti-Classic work.

CHICAGO ARCHITECTURAL PHOTOGRAPHING CO.

244 EAST 32nd STREET   NEW YORK 16, N Y   MURRAY HILL 4-4534

phonetic WRITING

Saturday

DEC 17 1958

Dear Philip:

        I just read your Sullivan article in the Art News (what
a disagreeable publication, I found again) and I liked it enormously.
I find it somewhat disturbing that the few of us who right architectural criticism nowadays - I think of Paul Rudolph's recent article
in the Record, your piece and my forthcoming reprint of my lecture
in PA - are in such accord that it all looks like mutual plagiarism
although it is just the opposite.

        There are two objections on my part to the Sullivan
piece. One is your statement:"Then it has a top. Why? It seemed
..."functional" to Sullivan; but hardly to us." I come more and
more to the conviction that the lack of " a top" is one of the most
serious shortcomings of modern design. There is a psychological
need for termination, for delineation. Paul das Wunderkind with
his godawful prismic skylights at Wellesley FEELS it but can't
design it. But nevertheless it is a real need. Everytime I get
in "my appointed rounds" at Pratt to 1420 and the unbelievably
beautiful cornice line of the Foundling Hospital, I feel as
if I had been delivered from a torture rack (visibly) after all
the gawking pinnacles and crockets and turrets and Fleches and
spires of the Gothic. (There always comes the awkward moment of
having to defend the blind loggia on the Pazzi on the same grounds
on which the Hospital is great; but it is only a moment of
embarrassment to be tided over with a fervent plea for the
"creative crises"of the genius.....)

I mean - Sullivan's **insis**tence on the Cornice is intuitively
right and for me there is a very touching evidence of this
struggle in him for the conciliation of the endlessly vertical and
the human horizontal in the treatment of the cornice frieze in
the Wainright and the Guaranty. The Wainright, 3 stories lower,
has still an embroidered piece of dodad decoration. Four years
later that frieze has become adjusted to the outward sweep of the
projecting rim as if it were a Byzantine mosaic.

My other objection is your statement that after the Guaranty Bldg.
Sullivan created nothing of worth and that his fenestration became
arbitrary and ill-proportioned. I think the relationship of the
rounded corner to the flat wall in Carson Pirie is excellent, no
matter how much he loused up the first two stories, and I always
stand in admiration before the Farmer's Bank at Owatonna. I think
the relationship of mass to perforation in that one is superb - mo
matter how dreary is the interior or how impotent the late successor to
it - the bank in Sidney from 1917.

Please forgive the unsolicited comments. I simply love to take you dreadfully serious when you talk about our common love.

The program of the SAH is so infinitely better than that of the College Art Association that I am very much playing with the idea of going out there for 1½ days. I haven't seen the GM Center, you know. Well, I'll report to you afterwards and you will confirm that it was a waste of time.

I do hope to see you during this oncoming vacation. I'll phone next weekend to see how things are.

December 19, 1956

Mrs. Sibyl Moholy-Nagy
244 East 32nd Street
New York 16, New York

Dear Sibyl:

I like your comment on my Sullivan and I agree with you
about the top of Sullivan's buildings, they are what made
him a great architect. And I agree with you about need-
ing tops on today's buildings. I think we have one on
Seagrams. What I meant was that we don't feel the necessity of a "cornice" like Sullivan did. We need cornices
too, but not heavy masonry ones like Sullivan's

I am sorry that I can't agree about Carson, Pirie. I
think it stinks. The same for the Bank.

Please go to the SAH meeting and report to me.

                    As ever,

                    Philip Johnson

PJ:mam

F.Ll.W. and the ageing of modern architecture

by Sibyl Moholy-Nagy

The fall-out of genius, good or evil, is absorbed involuntarily by mankind. Hitler, Einstein, Freud, Picasso have affected our existence without personal contact, and scores of volumes have been written to denounce or acclaim their power. The imprint of *architectural* revolutions on the individual life is stronger, more immediate than any political or ideological pressure, yet it would be a most exceptional consumer of architectural form and space who would feel the need of addressing an architectural innovator: "Sir, I owe you much of my visual vocabulary and physical environment. The time has come to tell you how I feel about your influence!" Few would care, because buildings have an unalterable finality. They are accepted like predestination. This lack of architectural criticism deprives culture of two important ingredients: it lets the positive achievement vegetate unnoticed, without the ultimate joy that could be derived from it; and it lets failure spawn failure because inadequacies remain undetected.

The critic who has decided to offer his qualified devotion to the late Giant of the Taliesins finds himself exposed to a surprise—a fact so unanticipated that it bears out the earlier assertion that we are all sheep dwelling blindly. There is a sudden realization that the modern architecture of today, and Modern Architecture as a movement, can neither be identified nor judged in the same terms. By its semantic root the word "modern" means "just now"; but Shakespeare interpreted it as "Things supernatural and causeless made modern and familiar." These different definitions of as simple a word as *modern* contain the whole conflict between the Founders of Modern Architecture and their heirs. One evaluation implies relentless actuality, the other a concretization of values transcendental; or, on the one side, modern architecture justified by material progress and, on the other, Modern Architecture justified on grounds of personal vision.

Frank Lloyd Wright decided for the Shakespearean definition of *modern* almost as soon as he raised his own pencil. After he had shed both the tutelage of Louis Sullivan, so clearly evident in the 1894 playroom of his Oak Park house **1**, and the commission-hungry opportunism indicated by the 1892 Blossom House **2**, he never again presented any of his work without a transcendental message, linking it to Christianity, Ethnography, Democracy, Humanism. Anyone even superficially familiar with his multitudinous writing knows these invocations:

"Architecture I know to be a Great Spirit. It can never be something that consists of the buildings which have been built by man on earth. . . . Any building is a by-product of eternal living force. It is in architecture that God meets with nature in the sphere of the relative."

"The Kingdom of God is within You—it seemed to me that organic architecture was the only visible evidence of this."

This spiritual substructure of Wright's work forms one of the most conspicuous links between him and his peers, Le Corbusier and Mies van der Rohe. All three transcendentalized their design, and it is doubtful that God has ever been invoked so frequently in any profession outside the church. One only has to recall Mies van der Rohe's intense preoccupation with St. Augustine and his "God is in the details," or Le Corbusier's comment on his low-cost Domino Houses from 1915, ". . . beautiful, thanks to a soul which artistic creativity has given to these austere and pure organisms," and the Cartesian skyscrapers, 60 floors high, ". . . which allow the inhabitants to savor the good things which a bountiful God dispenses to man."

The Modern Movement in architecture was conceived as a religion with but one true prophet possible among the three patriarchs who challenged each other's states of grace like the three counter-popes in the 14th Century. When Wright said recently to his representative on the Guggenheim Museum site, "Bill, they will still try to figure this one out a thousand years from now!" he knew himself the possessor of the Architectural Tablets, revealed only to him.

What did the revealed truth of "things supernatural and causeless" in architecture "modern and familiar" do for Wright's design and therefore for us? It gave America an *American* architecture and Western Civilization at large the proof that residential design can be both modern and intensely personal. If one accepts as the prerequisite of the title Genius, a contribution of unprecedented originality, then Wright's claim to genius lies with his autochthonous design of the house. Through his architectural

1

expression of the land, he raised regionalism to a new level, far above the sentimentality of Voysey or McKim. Never before had an architect been so fired by love for his country and his people. Out of this love he proposed to take on the whole subcontinent as inspiration and

May 12, 1959

Dear Sibyl,

I liked your piece on FLlW. I thought your analysis
of the transcendentalists of that day was excellent.
Hope you won't be too hard on those of us today who
don't always use structure expressively. I feel,
though I may be wrong, that you are going all out to
Nervi and Candela and company, and not being very
sympathetic with those of us trying to make ~~viable~~ Viable
forms for ordinary buildings. For instance, by
ordinary I mean trabeated construction since, as you
know, you cannot walk on hyperbolic paraboloids.

As you can imagine, I was not very pleased by your
article on modern art, but there is no point in friends
always agreeing.

I have been all over the country and haven't had a
night to myself since God knows when, but we must meet
before you get off for the summer.

As ever,

Mrs. Sibyl Moholy-Nagy
244 East 32nd Street
New York 17, New York

244 EAST 32nd STREET   NEW YORK 16, N Y   MURRAY HILL 4-4534

May 15, 1959

Dear Philip:

How nice of you to write me a note about the Wright piece in PA.
But how COULD you derive the impression that I am "going all out to Nervi
and Candela and company".... Quite, and quite emphatically, to the countrary!
All I wanted to point out was the non-esoteric basis of today's fashionable
artforms in architecture, the fact that even the fanciest millinery of Nervi
was arrived at from a materialistic point of departure. I might have sounded
less critical than I meant to be for the simple reason that I waded through such
reams of mystical doubletalk by both Le Corbusier and Wright in gathering material
for this piece, that ~~~~~ Mies' reticence and the absence of "contents" in
contemporary work seemed a great relief.

Relief it might be - but it certainly is no solution. I caused the
other night at the Architectural League a moment of embarrassment so thick, that
you could have sliced it with a mat knife: this was the evening"honor of Nervi.
Burchardt was at his most unbearable and Sweeney labored mightily in the vinyards
of imagism. Lejko glorified the architectural genius ; and when it was all done
Ketchum had the unfortunate idea to ask me to the microphone to say something about
Nervi. This I did - "and not without relish" to quote Churchill in quite another
context; and I said simply that I did not consider vaults, no matter how stunning,
architecture for the simple reason that they do not produce architectural space
on the one hand, and must needs lack architectural proportion in relationship to
the space consumer on the other. Well, it just wasn't the right thing at a
$ 5. - dinner - except for a handful of renegades who applauded frantically.
My whole brain and my whole heart are in arcuation (so damned rare) and good
"viable" (a lovely word the way you used it) trabeation. And as for "expressed
structure", that's as you know a long and complicated story.

I am in the throws of end semester at Pratt and terribly overworked at
the moment. But the end is in sight: May 26. I'll be in New Milford for about
5 weeks before going to South America around July 10th. It would be very nice
to have a meal and a long talk with you, either in town or out in the country; but
it's you who has to call me. My New Milford number is Elgin 4-5912.

Best as always -

Mark Morris

teaches architectural design and theory at Cornell University Department of Architecture. He is author of Models: Architecture and the Miniature *and* Automatic Architecture: Designs from the Fourth Dimension. *His dissertation tutor at the Architectural Association was Mark Cousins who studied with Ernst Gombrich at the Warburg Institute. Mark's research focuses on architectural models, scale, and questions of representation.*

Regarding *Regarding*

Seeing depends on knowledge
And knowledge, of course, on your college
But when you are erudite and wise
What matters is to use your eyes.

Ernst Gombrich

Architect at work from *Catalogue modèle de l'architecte,* 1913 (Paris, France). Courtesy of the Division of Rare and Manuscript Collections, Cornell University Libraries.

From its Anglo-French origins, *regarding* is defined as attentive looking, gazing in a specified fashion, or paying particular attention. Its Old French derivation also implies watching, guarding, and *looking back at.* As modes of seeing go, regarding is a proactive sort of vision overlaid with judgment. In so many ways, the capacity to regard is fundamental to the identity of the architect.

A pedagogy of regarding, if one can call it that, within an architectural curriculum owes something to art criticism, which shares architecture's preoccupation with visual analysis. Ernst Gombrich would be the salient figure and link between these disciplines. His work from *Art and Illusion* to *The Image and the Eye* sought a formal or rational study of art through optical and psychological study as opposed to art history or a quest for a zeitgeist. His inclusion of a few architectural examples, alongside artwork in his lectures and books, expanded the scope of his research and his audience. As an Andrew D. White professor-at-large at Cornell from 1970 to 1977, Gombrich brought his methods and techniques to students and interested faculty, Colin Rowe being one of them, in a series of lectures and interviews. Rowe was familiar with Gombrich through Rudolf Wittkower. Gombrich espoused the training of the eye and the mind to interrogate form and look for patterns, dissonance, alignments, aberrations, visual quotation, part-to-whole relationships, compositions of solid versus void, and genre-specific attributes. In short, he advocated a way of seeing now familiar to architects, and this familiarity is, in part, owed to his advocacy and interdisciplinary approach.

In order that we might better understand the characteristics of regarding, it is necessary to supplement Gombrich's thinking with a review of philosophical perspectives on the nature of perception. Regarding is a form of exteroception, the means by which we gain knowledge of the world outside ourselves through our five senses; sight, in this case. It requires subjectivity and objectivity, internal and external awareness. In *Critique of Pure Reason* Immanuel Kant sets up the dichotomy of intensive and extensive quantities of perception. Intensive is aligned with intuition, extensive is aligned with perception based on sensation. He acknowledges a kind of apprehension, aligned with intuition, not dependent on sensation: "All cognition, by means of which I am enabled to cognize and determine a priori what belongs to empirical cognition, may be called an Anticipation..."[1] Perception is the combination of anticipation and sensation; substantiating the claim that to see something you have to be looking for it in the first place.

Descartes, however, has other notions of vision that are indispensable to the question of perception: "all the objects of sight communicate themselves to us only through the fact that they move locally *by* the intermission of transparent bodies which are between them and us...."[2] We neither see objects as they are (extensive) nor as we are (intensive), but as something produced in between as a result of the tension caught between these types of quantities. These transparent bodies are translators of visual information and this translation takes place, Descartes imagines, in the fluid of the eyeball, a funneling of the world through the wet optic vestibule en route to the mind.

The mind's interpretation of this information permits it to form judgments, good and bad. Descartes writes of deception (bad perception) as having two possible triggers: appearance and judgment about something based on appearance or, to put it another way, misapprehension and misjudgment.[3] Misjudgment is the more powerful outcome according to Descartes. He relates it to the case of the phantom limb, where the patient imagines pain in a lost arm or leg; the feeling of pain is real and the judgment assumes that the limb is there. Vivid dreams, likewise, offer appearances that may lead to erroneous judgments. Hallucination, or a waking dream, is required to support imagined things; the misjudgment must be met by misapprehension in this equation. An architect's ability to creatively explore "in the mind's eye" is a form of hallucination whereby something is visualized based on a supposition that may be purely speculative. "Realizing one's vision," finding a way to build the hallucinated design (every academic project, every competition; in short, every architectural proposal), is a process of post-rationalization of hallucination that is ultimately a working definition of architecture as a creative practice.

Internal vision, creativity, is more than insight or proprioception. It is a phase beyond any perception where the mind alone, equipped with the memory of so many images, can amalgamate, fracture, reconcile, or layer images to produce something new and hold that assemblage long enough to export it in the form of some representation; a drawing, for example. When Rowe evokes Claude Lévi-Strauss's use of the term *bricoleur* and writes that "artistic creation lies mid-way between science and bricolage,"[4] he joins internal vision and scientific observation as the circuit, not the dialectic, of any architectural endeavor. Architects individually may be assigned the label of bricoleur or engineer, but, for Rowe, this dichotomy is merely illustrative of the creative process running in different directions: "the scientist and the 'bricoleur' are to be distinguished 'by the inverse functions which they assign to event and structures as a means and ends, the scientist creating events ... by means of structures and the 'bricoleur' creating structures by means of events.'"[5] Each drives the other.

The bricoleur relies on "a set of tools and materials which is always infinite and is also heterogeneous because what it contains bears no relation to the current project, or indeed to any particular project, but is the contingent result of all the occasions there have been to renew or enrich the stock or to maintain it with the remains of previous constructions or destructions."[6] The *stock* is an archive of images and recollection of experiences that can be raided to answer any project brief. One's power to draw from multiple precedents, to form a fresh response with the DNA of everything they have previously noted as memorable, is one's stance as a bricoleur. A precedent study at the start of a design project is a strategic means to *enrich the stock*. This process of massaging the memory with precedents to aid internal vision is part of the looking back inference of regarding. Maintaining this stock involves looking at architecture firsthand (traveling) and secondhand in books and journals, in class as projections, and so on, and looking at it in a way that constructively transfers to memory.

Perception is, therefore, not seeing, but thinking through what one has seen and stored in memory. Rudolf Arnheim claims, "All perceiving is also thinking, all reasoning is also intuition, all observation is also invention."[7] Descartes concurs: "Perception … is neither a seeing, nor a touching, nor an imagining…rather it is an inspection on the part of the mind alone."[8] John Miller extends the argument for perception being fueled by but detached from literal vision in his *Metaphysics or the Sciences of Perception*. Perception is defined as "a grand phenomenon of the conscious current," having three aspects: consciousness, emotion, and cognition. "Not only is all Consciousness Perception, that is, every conscious gaze a perceiving, and all of it a perceiving of that that we are conscious of, but all Perception is conscious."[9] Miller links perception to emotion and pleasure in part because it permits abstraction and analysis. Architects know this pleasure; they may be addicted to it.

The "conscious gaze" is inverted by Jacques Lacan who locates consciousness in the object being gazed at rather than the subject. This is an extension and reworking of Freud's claim that one might project a fear or desire on an object; *project* being the optimum word linking thought, vision, and the architectural sense of project or work resulting from visual thoughts. Such a psychoanalytic proposition sits comfortably with architects who may imagine that their work holds something of their perception or represents their way of seeing the world. To even think such a thing, a Lacanian breakthrough must transpire, a moment when the architects realize that they are looking at things in a particular way. This epiphany is the result of retraining the eye to regard rather than merely see things, to store them in memory (looking back) and then abstract and analyze them on demand. All this feeds that particular brand of creativity architecture values: not whim, not pure originality, but thoughtful synthesis of known elements deployed for new purposes. The role of originality is to blend the stock with a unique capacity for abstraction so the known elements are not clearly deciphered *as with a collage*. The capacity for such measured abstraction is rooted in one's powers of analysis, making the specific portable and mutable.

Since Lacan's death in 1981, a broad-based shift in visual preoccupation was prompted by a mechanism useful for transferring and holding images. The computer has altered architects' visual training and crafting of representations to be regarded by others. Faculty and students at Cornell were at the forefront of advancing the visuality of computation, their contributions notably embodied in the so-called Cornell Box. Functioning as a proof and claim for virtuality, the green, red, and white cabinet could be filled with objects—cubes, spheres, mirrors—and its photographed image compared to a computer rendering of a virtual double. The aim was to check the capacity of software applications to accurately represent not only the objects but calculate their interreflections and shadows. Accuracy was assumed to be beneficial, but figures like Stan Allen would take exception to the premise that the digital should strive toward photorealism, "it ignores what has traditionally given architectural representation its particular power of conceptualization—that is to say, its necessary degree of abstraction, the distance imposed between the thing and its representation."[10] *The distance imposed* harkens back to the Cartesian gap between the physical thing and its image as perceived. This is the space of regarding or the gap where regarding figuratively operates. And it happens all the time on the computer when software is used heuristically, diagrammatically, analytically, or as Allen puts it, "used against the grain" of its intended mimetic function.

The more substantive shift in perception under the auspices of the digital has less to do with the quality of images and more to do with quantity. Image searches on the internet have replaced a whole culture of visual research previously grounded in hard-copy access provided by libraries and print media; the slide being a virtual and literally projective auxiliary. Gombrich's carefully selected and sequenced slides had time to settle on the retina and be committed to memory as a byproduct of their persistence in the visual field. The same temporal dynamic is not easily recaptured in the flit between a search engine's results that display as slides on a light table, but when selected singly struggle to manage the same critical work as their magic lantern forbears, in part owing to their variable resolution, cropping, and color saturation. More problematic is the selection itself based on popularity rather than architectural eligibility. Images are not all equally useful. If regarding is defined as attentive looking, it cannot be said that Google gives rise to an alternative sensibility of regarding. It simply does something else.

Contemporary architectural critics come back to the question of apprehension through historic case studies. When Rosalind Krauss critiques Ruskin's claims that neglect and lack of toys in childhood forced him to become a keen observer and generate "that capacity for attention so pure and so disinterested," she admits, "Ruskin's view-hunting is a means of transforming the whole of nature into a machine for producing images, establishing in this way an autonomous field of the visual—characterized, indeed, by those two qualities onto which the optical sense opens uniquely: the infinitely multiple on the one hand, and the simultaneously unified on the other."[11] The multiple refers to attention to detail, and the unified aspect refers to the power of abstraction. In this way, Allen's concern about the saturation of detail in digital renderings is answered by acknowledging only through fastidious looking at details—their multiplicity, density, diverse scales—can meaningful abstraction be distilled. Krauss describes this obsessive scopic grazing as Ruskin's *luxuriant stare*. Gombrich, building his own case for visual training, credited Ruskin's assertion that reading an image requires an education.

Philibert de l'Orme, **The Bad Architect and The Good Architect**, the first volume of architecture *(Le premier tome de l'architecture)*, 1567. Courtesy of the Division of Rare and Manuscript Collections, Cornell University Libraries.

The connotation of regarding as a form of guarding is the most etymologically obvious. It suggests that to really look at something without too much distraction is to guard, preserve, and conceptually protect something with all that perception implies. Architects guard things by looking at them, thinking about and through images, and making more images in kind. The creation of images is dependent on the careful looking and archiving of many more. The archive is guarded by memory and strengthened by frequent additions and raiding for the purposes of creativity. The capacity to regard is fundamental to the identity of the architect, and this also plays out visually. Philibert de l'Orme's architectural 16th-century allegories show the "bad architect" without eyes or hands wandering a dry landscape and the "good architect" in a classical garden teaching a student. De l'Orme gives the good architect four hands and three eyes, the third eye being an eye for wise seeing.

Le Corbusier's iconic eyeglasses remain a sign of the architect and his perceptual prowess. The glasses suggest the eyes have been exhausted by professional commitment. They also literally frame the world and objectify the discipline, intimating that anyone who wears them might see as an architect sees. This trope remains popular with architects: Philip Johnson, Louis Kahn, Eero Saarinen, Peter Eisenman, I.M. Pei, Toyo Ito, Rafael Vinoly, Peter Cook, Daniel Libeskind, Nicholas Grimshaw, Wolf Prix, and so on. A next generation faithfully copies this group, even in an age of contact lenses and laser eye surgery. But there are no magic glasses that instantly produce an architect. Rather, it takes a particular education dedicated to retraining the eye, lengthening attention spans, and testing the retention of visual information to produce one. Regarding remains an unusual expertise and one that may still deserve undistracted attention. This seems a skill worth guarding.

Instant Architect, a favorite image of the architecture blogosphere, courtesy of Archinect.

Instruction:
1. Cut out pieces
2. Attach Tab A to B
3. Wa-Lah!

Endnotes

1 Immanuel Kant, *Critique of Pure Reason*, James Creed Meredith (trans.) (Oxford: Oxford University Press, 1952), 180.

2 *The Philosophical Works of Descartes*, Elizabeth S. Haldane and G.R.T. Ross (trans.) (New York and London: Cambridge University Press, 1970), XV:13.

3 Ibid.

4 Colin Rowe and Fred Koetter, *Collage City* (Cambridge: MIT Press, 1984), 103.

5 Ibid.

6 Ibid., 102.

7 Rudolf Arnheim, *Art and Visual Perception* (Berkeley and Los Angeles: University of California Press, 1974), 5.

8 *The Philosophical Works of Descartes,* II:2.

9 John Miller, *Metaphysics or the Sciences of Perception* (New York: Dodd and Mead, 1877), 30.

10 Stan Allen, "Terminal Velocities: The Computer in the Design Studio," in *The Virtual Dimension: Architecture, Representation and Crash Culture*, John Beckmann (ed.) (New York: Princeton Architectural Press, 1998), 246.

11 Rosalind Krauss, *The Optical Unconscious*, 5th ed. (London and Cambridge, MA: MIT Press, 1998), 6.

A-Locations/Pre-Occupations

John Zissovici

Aboriginal Creation myths te
legendary totemic beings w
wandered over the continer
Dreamtime, singing out the
everything that crossed their
. . . rocks, waterholes —
singing the world into exi

. . . the constructed nature of its

"Already . . . in advance, the image owed something to this moment."[2]

The mythical landscape of the twentieth century can be thought of as the vast fields and streams of images of the world, into which the reality of the world has been transformed in the media. Through the persuasive and pervasive repetitiveness with which society proliferates representations of its values, the mythical landscape of modern life has acquired its own naturalness. The rocks and waterholes of the old myth have been replaced by signs and representations. As technical and scientific progress allows for the unlimited transformation of nature, technology – the mechanism through which the world as image is perpetually reaffirmed by the media – is revealed to be both perpetrator and hidden ground of our mythical landscape, this 'second nature'.[3]

"Myths [today] are nothing but this ceaseless . . . insidious and inflexible demand that all men recognize themselves in this image . . . which was built of them one day as if for all time. For the Nature, in which they are locked up under the pretext of being eternalized is nothing but a Usage. And it is this Usage, however lofty, that they must take in hand and transform."[4]

The interruption of the endless flow of images and the appropriation of a fragment of this new landscape for closer examination, reflect both the central concern and field of operation of the architectural problem. The explorations of this fragment aim to expose the constructed nature

Splitting, Gordon Matta-Clark, 1974

Fig. 1

of its reality, and its subsequent relocation within the framework of architectural production is set before the students as the focus of the studio.

The projects start out by taking one of two photographs of 'lost' objects and transposing it into an 'accounting', a dramatic discursive action that builds upon the image's internal structure by retracing the paths of its becoming. While this exercise seems to solve no immediate problems (the projects merely fill the void that precedes their existence), expansive mappings enable the ambiguities between the object and the representation to emerge in concrete form. Through speculative proposals for the occupation of these forms the projects mirror the formations of myths, and so become predictive myths "that you can actually live by: how to cope with . . . the whole series of enciphered meanings that lie half-exposed within the urban landscape, within the communication landscape we all inhabit and to some extent contribute to."[5] Like all myths, they stand as "exemplary models for all significant human activity."[6] Their lessons are like an after-image, a reverberation of all that has been set in motion. Our engagement, or reading of these projects, can be seen as a ritual re-enacting, an active participation in the myth.

Each student begins with one of two images of lost ships, victims of man-made and natural disasters. These are put forth to challenge investigations into the nature and role of representation in the context of a 'museum/monument' as well as in the architectural production.

Fig. 2

Dear John,

In issue 4 of The Cornell Journal of Architecture, *your text, "A-Locations / Pre-Occupations" described the "mythical landscape of the twentieth century" as a landscape transformed by the media of images and signs. In the 20 years since the publication of that issue, the century's clock has moved on, and with it, the role of the image in our world has proliferated to the extreme. The question for you is simple:*

*Mythical landscapes of the twenty-*first *century?*

—Eds.

John Zissovici

is associate professor at Cornell University Department of Architecture, where he teaches, practices, and researches new technologies and their relationship to architecture and the city.

SurfaceCities

Renovating the Image of the 21st-Century City

> *I say therefore that likeness or thin shapes*
> *Are sent out from the surfaces of things*
> *Which we must call as it were their film or bark*
> *Because the image bears the look and shape*
> *Of the body from which it came, as it floats in the air.*
>
> T. Lucretius Carus, *De Rerum Natura*, first-century B.C.

Lucretius's notion of high-speed atomic particles that emanate from objects and enter the eyes to cause vision and visualization is an apt topological model for the mediated, pixelated nature of our current condition. Today, digital images of the city on the luminous liquid crystal display screens of mobile communication devices have acquired a similar role to his "likeness" in visualizing the city. To understand vision as "seeing" (the city) through the mediating images on the screen confers the digital image the same elevated status as Lucretius's "thin shapes." The digital image has become the necessary transitional state of things before they enter our consciousness; that is, the image on the screen is the precondition for visualizing the city.

The cumulative effect of this increasingly mediated experience is to temporarily transform the city itself into an imagescape, a "reality-effect … a dissociated system, a puzzle the observer [is] unable to solve without some traffic in light or the appropriate prosthesis … and to demonstrate … 'mechanically' that man should experience the world as an illusion of the world."[1] The prosthetic hand-held mobile communication device with its glowing LCD screen is the device that solves the puzzle of the city. It is also the medium for reimagining it.

Contrary to the city seen through the mirrors and lenses of the viewfinder of an analog camera, the digital city as it appears on the LCD screen is already a supplemental layer, an excess manifestation of the city, which can only exist temporarily in the real time and space of the city. This transient digital image of the city is also open to being augmented by other image layers before it enters our consciousness.

These new image layers correspond to whatever view appears on the LCD screen as it can now be linked to the original image irrespective of camera orientation. This phenomenon, called augmented reality, originally seen on TV in 1998 as the virtual yellow first-down line, was the initial intrusion of the virtual into the "real" image world. The effect of the stable yellow line within shifting perspectives is made possible by digitally linking the various broadcasting cameras to a virtual field that is "aligned" to the actual field of play.

The yellow line, which changes position as the teams move back and forth across the field, is located and "drawn" on the virtual field, then superimposed onto the image of the actual field. This enhancement of the televised image created the illusion for the TV audience that the movable yellow line was actually on the field, but in fact was invisible to the spectators at the game. The ubiquitous virtual yellow line is by now an integral part of all NFL games broadcast on TV.

Augmented reality, however, is a term that wrongly and unfairly reduces the digital image's role in making reality more real: wrongly because it assumes the mere augmentation of an image of reality, and unfairly because it fails to capture the full potential of the image as an integral part of experience. (All NFL fields are now equipped with multiple giant screens that display the real-time televised image with the virtual yellow first-down marker.) At the same time this phenomenon is still widely seen as a lamentable condition, a devaluation of the "real" at the expense of the "authentic," mainly attributed to the commercialization of the public sphere. This point of view contributes to the divisive, dead-end, this-or-that, architecture-or-its-representation discussion and fails to acknowledge the extent to which the mediating digital image is not merely a precondition for "seeing," but has already been absorbed into everyday experience.

Detour

Rome, the unlikely model for the future city, provides an unexpected example of the dynamic way in which images have come to insinuate themselves into the fabric of the city and its citizens' lives. The proliferation of idealized full-scale images of facades in front of buildings was initially a pragmatic response to the problem of having large numbers of Rome's buildings in the historic center under renovation, hidden from the eyes of expectant tourists. Stretched over construction scaffolding, the silk-screened images on scrim—replacements for the ubiquitous cheap green protective nylon mesh—appear as masks, temporary substitutes for the facades.

To pay for the expensive and expansive images, themselves often advertisements for pristine future historic facades, and to defray the cost of the actual renovation, a certain percentage of the image facade is allowed to be occupied by income-producing advertising.

The setup of scrim with picture-in-picture images, its supporting scaffolding that structures the space of renovation, and the veiled building facade hiding the building's occupants, is a mise-en-scène endlessly repeated around Rome, temporarily suggesting the image of modern cities like New York or Tokyo, but still uniquely analog, low-tech, and Roman.

Grafted onto the building's mask is the ever-changeable advertising chip that records the city's shifting taste in fashion, art, politics, and inevitably religion. Meanwhile, the mask allows the face/facade to remain expressionless, a true reflection of Rome's generally stoic response to the often turbulent interaction between the forces that use the city as their background.

The graft/augmentation starts out as the inset stretched canvas, the implied movie screen, all promise and potential. The duration of its blank state seems to follow no discernible pattern, turning expectation into its own spectacle. Nothing will ever be projected here except the shadow of the lights intended to confer on any future image eternal visibility.

This being Rome, the tensions between the graft, the mask, and the face are most evident when churches are involved. The first advertisement in Rome announcing the coming of the film version of *The Da Vinci Code* appears within the image of

the church of San Pantaleo. Over a close-up of Leonardo's *La Gioconda,* her mouth covered by a triangle of texture, is written, "This is how they obscure the language of man." A few days later, after strenuous objection by the Vatican and much debate in the press, the image was replaced by a funerary black scrim with a satanic morphing moiré effect. On closer inspection, it is evident that the original image was merely turned inside out to face the interior of the church, as if impossibly rotated around the central seam. An even more subversive reminder of *Il codice da Vinci,* now spelled backward and barely visible still haunts the Piazza San Pantaleo.

Meanwhile, inset into the mask of an apartment building on the Largo Argentina, a mere five blocks away, a new, more secular-looking ad for the movie appears overnight, and remains in place for the duration of the film's showing. This new graft, transformed suddenly from its months-long state of whiteness, now appears to have been poised as a strategic trump card in a long-anticipated war. The battle for the hearts and minds of the people of Rome is played out in/on images, in real time and real space. As the presence of the bright yellow bus advertising "Tours of Christian Rome" suggests, the bland image of Tom Hanks with his French co-star, as well as the censored blackness in the mask of San Pantaleo, have already been absorbed as contemporary detours updating the city's Christian history.

This ongoing dynamic urban spectacle plays itself out in the image projected from the city's historic facades into the contemporary public sphere. The surplus space created by the projection accommodates the work needed to maintain the illusion of Rome's eternity.

The persistence of this multifunctional infrastructure for simulation, communication, and labor, well beyond the few-years-long rush to renovate Rome's decaying image for the millennium, attests to its integration into the enduring image of the city and all facets of its public life.

With the partial disappearance of countless buildings behind their own representations, the city, its image, and its inhabitants must now be reimagined in real time, on site, building by building, as one moves through the city encountering the scrimmed ghosts of blurred lives and buildings. Each building under renovation, with its excess imagery and space, acts as a trigger for speculation.

APPliedCITY

The LCD image in the city renders every point in the city into a potentially mediated experience and temporarily transforms the city into a mediated field of actions. Like its Roman and pre-Roman precedents, the potentially layered image on the LCD screen is now inserted and experienced in the city in real time and on location, merely by turning the device on. Because of its small size, the screen image is never immersive, never replaces the city, which surrounds it. It is a digital pixel of, and within, the larger world, now with the power to contribute to the creation of an alternative landscape of image surfaces.

Because each image is also a directional view from a specific location, it can be linked to countless supplemental layers of images, texts, and numbers selected to contribute to the image space of the city. Each applied new layer starts out as a virtual framework, a schematic version of the city, like the virtual "field" on which the yellow line is drawn, that is constantly realigned with the city and its digital image on the screen. New layers are selected manifestations of these APPliedCITIES and can be overlaid onto the plan, displayed with the screen in the horizontal position or as views with the screen held vertically. Movement between these two modes of representation is as simple as rotating the device from the horizontal to the vertical position.

The actual city is a joystick for navigating the virtual realm, as movement through the physical city is translated into movement through the APPliedCITY, made possible by various tracking technologies. Scripting the relation between the scale of movement in the actual city and its virtual counterpart allows movement by foot, bicycle, car, subway, or even vertically by elevator, to correspond to all scales and axes of movement in a parallel virtual model. For the moment, the most radical inversion necessary for reimagining our relationship to the city takes place as the city becomes instrumental in accessing parallel virtual realms linked to it.

The TEXT APPliedCity exploits the actual city as an infrastructural surface for posting virtual message layers by its users, a spatialization of texting to correspond to the scale of the city. It would create new features and paths of reading, or identify unexpected locations of gathering for shared public virtual reading. These virtual surfaces could also be the first subliminal suggestion for transforming features of certain parts of the actual city. *Project by Roger Mainor and Anahita Rouzbeh.*

The HISTORIC APPliedCity superimposes previous actual and unrealized versions onto the image of the contemporary city as plans and views, both equally productive in speculating about the city over time. The device is able to record the movement of this APPliedCity's explorers into a cumulative, ever-changing map of attempts to retrace the historic layer. Along with the superimposed views, these would reveal spatial and temporal convergences or disjunctions with the contemporary city. *Project by Ryan Drummond.*

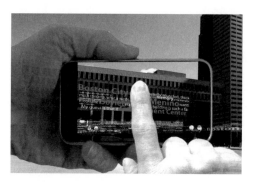

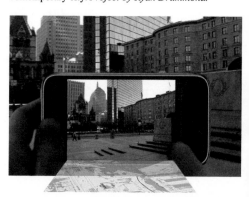

The SUBWAY APPliedCity would alleviate the spatial and sensorial deprivation of the subway journey by linking its trajectory to movement through a variety of parallel APPliedCities based on existing or fictional features of the unseen city. The static scene of the subway car would be enhanced by corresponding to virtual journeys through APPliedCITIES on the screen, alternative narratives, whose moments of intersection with the subterranean trip, recorded as virtual memories, would later be sought out for "verification" in the actual city. *Project by Sarah Haubner and Konrad Scheffer.*

The SKYSPHERE APPliedCITY is a social networking application that allows its users to generate a constantly mutating aerial panorama, virtually mirroring their city from above; a fluid record of their numbers and location, a reflection of shared paths and districts of participation. *Project by Xiaoben Dai and Moritz Schoendorf.*

As a receptacle for supplemental layers of images, a dynamic device for locating and navigating text-images in real time, on site, this new mediated city recalls an earlier role of the city as a mnemonic device, an ordering structure for a set of loci, physical locations where images are deposited for later recall. Yet in their more expansive role, mnemonic devices were also intended to aid in the combination of ideas that leads to invention. With its ability to combine layers of historic, analytic, and speculative images and data of the city drawn from an increasingly vast depository, the APPliedCITIES[2] are conduits to insights and discoveries, leading to infinitely varied discourses that alter the way the city is used, remembered, and therefore imagined. Like the temporally ambiguous scrim images of facades in Rome (are they a historic, pre-renovation record, or projective of a future state?), with their ever-changing advertising chip, the layered images on the screen expand the experience of the city into a multitude of temporal and spatial dimensions.

Each of these mediated experiences is centered on looking, *"an obsession in which real time is suspended while, as in dreams, the dead, the living and the still unborn come together on the same plane,"*[3] and creates its own unique layered set of memories of the city.

Each APPliedCITY is a mise en abyme of the actual city, a mise-en-scène of a new city. The insertion of the excess imagery disrupts our experience of the city, which is continually visible to us and allows us to reimagine it digitally.

The pervasive presence of digital images of the city within the urban environment links the digital and actual manifestations of the city into a constantly mutating, interdependent relationship that destabilizes the "real" versus "virtual" argument. Like in Rome, it is in the alternate (rather than augmented) reality of the space between the city and its image, that a renovation of the image/idea of the city can be performed. Unlike in Rome, the deployment and lifespan of the layered image on the LCD screen is fully in control of the individual user ready to disappear as soon as the device is turned off. The mediated city only really exists when seen on site, on the screen as an image. Its effect, however, like Rome, is likely to be eternal.

APPendix

Many of the ideas developed here come out of a graduate studio co-taught with Yanni Loukissas. Students proposed applications for mobile communication devices as a way to explore the impact of new technologies on the way we create images of cities, in contrast to Kevin Lynch's *The Image of the City* from 50 years ago. The images of APPliedCITIES are student projects developed in the studio.

Endnotes

1 Paul Virilio, *The Vision Machine* (Bloomington: Indiana University Press, 1994), 5.
2 SurfaceCities Studio, Department of Architecture, Cornell University, Fall 2009, http://www.surfacecities.com.
3 W.G. Sebald, *Campo Santo* (New York: Random House, 2005), 15.

125

Michael Ashkin

with Nathan Townes-Anderson

Michael Ashkin has exhibited nationally and internationally, including in Documenta 11 in 2002 and the Whitney Biennial in 1997. Most recently, in 2009, his work was the subject of a solo show at Secession in Vienna. Ashkin is currently director of graduate studies in the College of Architecture, Art, and Planning's Department of Art, at Cornell University.

Nathan Townes-Anderson is an artist and writer based in Ithaca, New York.

Resolution (Western Sahara)

THE SITUATION CONCERNING WESTERN SAHARA[141]

Decision

At its 2984th meeting, on 29 April 1991, the Council discussed the item entitled "The situation concerning Western Sahara: report by the Secretary-General (S/22464 and Corr.1)".[7]

Resolution 690 (1991)
of 29 April 1991

The Security Council,

Recalling its resolution 621 (1988) of 20 September 1988, by which it,
inter alia, requested the Secretary-General to transmit to it a report on the holding of a referendum for self-determination of the people of Western Sahara and on ways and means to ensure the organization and supervision of such a referendum by the United Nations in cooperation with the Organization of African Unity,

Recalling also that, on 30 August 1988, the Kingdom of Morocco and the Frente Popular para la Liberación de Saguía el-Hamra y de Río de Oro gave their agreement in principle to the proposals of the Secretary-General of the United Nations and the current Chairman of the Assembly of Heads of State and Government of the Organization of African Unity in the framework of their joint mission of good offices,

Recalling further its resolution 658 (1990) of 27 June 1990, by which it approved the report of the Secretary-General of 18 June 1990,[142] which contains the full text of the settlement proposals as accepted by the two parties on 30 August 1988, as well as an outline of the plan provided by the Secretary-General in order to implement those proposals, and by which it requested the Secretary-General to transmit to it a further detailed report on his implementation plan, containing in particular an estimate of the cost of the United Nations Mission for the Referendum in Western Sahara,

Desirous of reaching a just and lasting solution of the question of Western Sahara,

Having examined the report of the Secretary-General of 19 April 1991 on the situation concerning Western Sahara,[143]

1. *Approves* the report of the Secretary-General, transmitted to the Council in accordance with resolution 658 (1990);[143]

2. *Expresses its full support* for the efforts of the Secretary-General for the organization and the supervision, by the United Nations in cooperation with the Organization of African Unity, of a referendum for self-determination of the people of Western Sahara, in accordance with the objectives mentioned in his report;

3. *Calls upon* the two parties to cooperate fully with the Secretary-General in the implementation of his plan as described in his report of 18 June 1990[142] and amplified in his report of 19 April 1991;[143]

4. *Decides* to establish, under its authority, a United Nations Mission for the Referendum in Western Sahara in accordance with the report of 19 April 1991;

5. *Also decides* that the transitional period will begin no later than sixteen weeks after the General Assembly approves the budget for the Mission;

6. *Requests* the Secretary-General to keep the Security Council regularly informed of the implementation of his settlement plan.

Adopted unanimously at the 2984th meeting

Decisions

In a letter dated 21 June 1991[144] addressed to the President of the Security Council for the attention of the members of the Council, the Secretary-General referred to paragraph 82 of his report of 18 June 1990 on the situation concerning Western Sahara,[142] in which he had stated that he would seek the Council's consent to the appointment of the Force Commander of the Military Unit of the United Nations Mission for the Referendum in Western Sahara. Having completed his consultations with the parties, he proposed, with the consent of the Council, to appoint Major-General Armand Roy (Canada) as the Force Commander of the Military Unit of the Mission.

In a letter dated 24 June 1991,[145] the President of the Security Council informed the Secretary-General as follows:

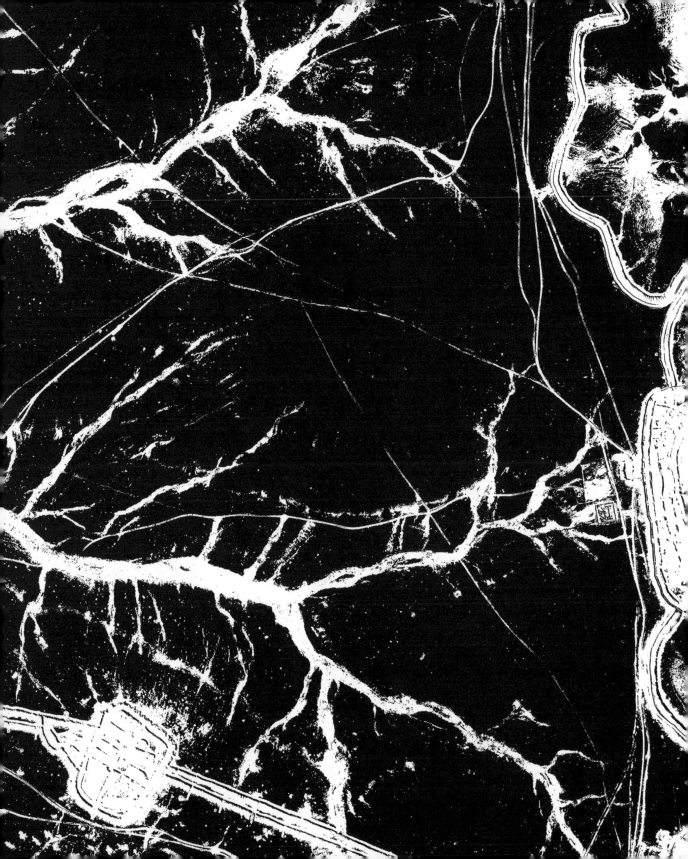

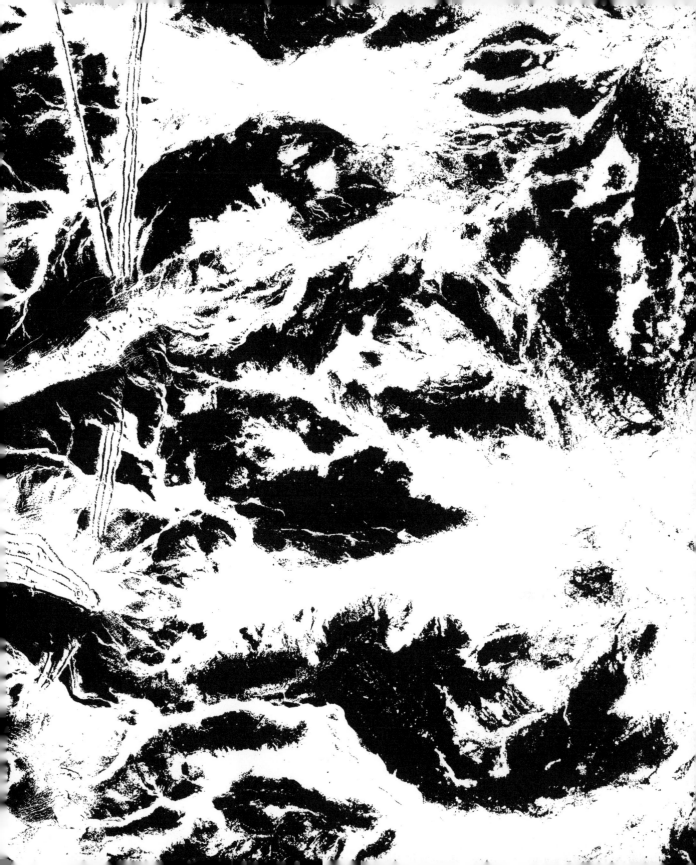

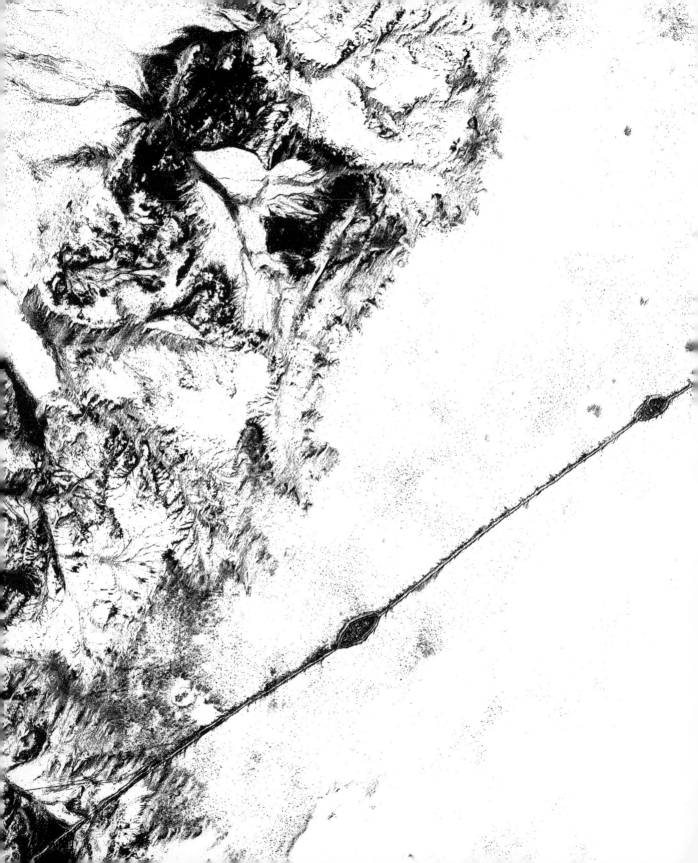

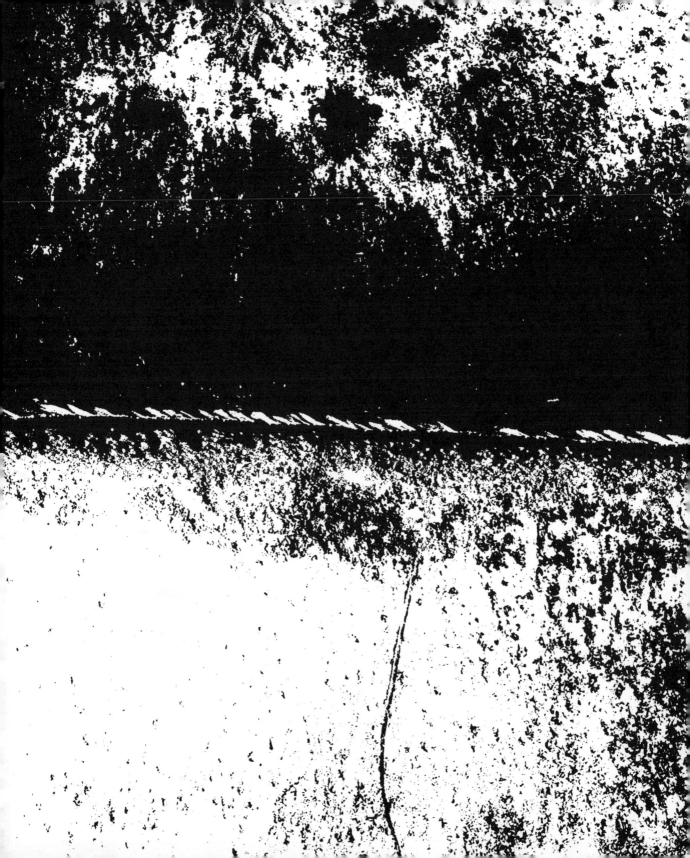

Resolution 1920 (2010)

Adopted by the Security Council at its 6305th meeting, on 30 April 2010

The Security Council,

Recalling and *reaffirming* all its previous resolutions on Western Sahara,

Reaffirming its strong support for the efforts of the Secretary-General and his Personal Envoy to implement resolutions 1754 (2007), 1783 (2007), 1813 (2008), and 1871 (2009),

Reaffirming its commitment to assist the parties to achieve a just, lasting, and mutually acceptable political solution, which will provide for the self-determination of the people of Western Sahara in the context of arrangements consistent with the principles and purposes of the Charter of the United Nations, and *noting* the role and responsibilities of the parties in this respect,

Reiterating its call upon the parties and States of the region to cooperate more fully with the United Nations and with each other to end the current impasse and to achieve progress towards a political solution,

Taking note of the Moroccan proposal presented on 11 April 2007 to the Secretary-General and welcoming serious and credible Moroccan efforts to move the process forward towards resolution; also *taking note* of the Polisario Front proposal presented 10 April 2007 to the Secretary-General,

Inviting in this context the parties to demonstrate further political will towards a solution,

Taking note of the four rounds of negotiations held under the auspices of the Secretary-General, and two rounds of informal talks held in Dürnstein (Austria) and Westchester County (United States) and *welcoming* the progress made by the parties to enter into direct negotiations,

Stressing the importance of making progress on the human dimension of the conflict as a means to promote transparency and mutual confidence through constructive dialogue and humanitarian confidence-building measures, and *noting* the need for all parties to adhere to their obligations, taking into account the roles and responsibilities of the UN system and the relevant paragraphs of the UN Secretary-General's report,

10-33942 (E)

 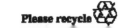

Dear Sabine and Andreas,
    In your project The Charter of Dubai, *which was presented as part of* Refuge *at the* International Architecture Biennale Rotterdam 2009, *you criticized up-market gated communities as a wasteful deception of independence. Using the completed Palm Jumeirah as the ultimate reference of the failed housing-market, you proposed a re-imagination of not what this icon could have been, but instead, just by reorienting resources latent in luxurious designs, you project what can be done now given the status quo. We invite you to articulate and develop this reconfiguration as a series of operations and attacks on the existing site.*
    —Eds.

SMAQ: Sabine Müller/Andreas Quednau

are a Berlin-based collaborative studio for architecture, urbanism, and research that focuses on urban design and architecture as a (re)active practice of "making something which cannot perform without the assistance of its environment." SMAQ has received, among other awards, the prestigious AR Award and the Holcim Award for Sustainable Construction. Sabine Müller is assistant professor of Architecture and Urban Design at Karlsruhe Institute of Technology, Germany. Andreas Quednau is professor of Architecture and Urban Design at Stuttgart State Academy of Art and Design, Germany.

Ex-Palm

This is a manifesto of urban readjustment, drafted at a moment when the global real-estate market has ground to a halt. We find ourselves left with the remains of an investment practice that thrives only on premium spaces: malls, business parks, gated communities, retreats, and resorts. Inevitably, the luxury refuges of today will be reclaimed for adapted use, integrated into the larger context of tomorrow's open city, and adjusted to the dynamics of the environment.

Why call these premium spaces *refuges?* It is evident that these spaces form enclaves that withdraw from the wider city, or from society altogether. The world over, these refuges have been legitimizing tendencies toward the development of a fragmented and socially stratified urbanity, which was pertinently described as *splintering urbanism* by Stephen Graham and Simon Marvin.[1] The self-contained resort is a subterfuge—a deception of independence—from which infrastructure and influence is extended across borders and boundaries undetected. In turn, resources are squandered at the expense and exclusion of others.

The task at hand: How to turn the refuge from a traditional burgh, a fortified town, into a *borough,* a quarter that is a functional and comprehensive part of the urban landscape?

The Palm Jumeirah, also called the Palm Dubai, is not only the most spectacular of upscale refuges; it is also the *paradigm:* the ultimate diagram in terms of figure, internal organization, and external relations. This is why it serves as both a case study of critique and a test for transformation. Several measures of transformation are explored on the Palm while synchronically leveraged as general principles applicable to any upscale refuge.

By addressing the structural logics of the refuge, the points of critique become stepping-stones of intervention and moreover provide opportunity for minimal incursions with major effects.

The methodology is based on the notion that luxury refuges built during the last real-estate boom present a massive societal investment in terms of capital, expertise, and labor. They have been built to speculate on a heated real-estate market. On the Palm, so-called virtual villas had been bought and resold ten times before the first stone was laid. Prices tripled, and when they fell suddenly, people with no real interest in using the homes called themselves owners. In the aftermath, the infrastructure (literally the earthwork, roads, cables, tubes, and building stock) is all that remains of these dysfunctional specters.

The infrastructural skeleton, stripped bare from the fattened values of an economy of attention and speculation, becomes the substance to be reworked.

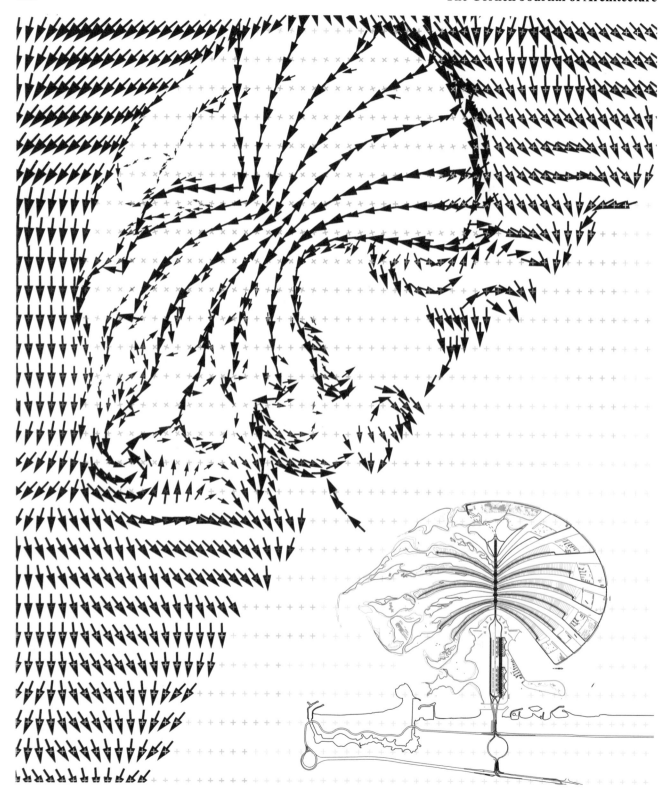

Re:form: From spectacular aerial icon to urban ground-scape figure
Contemporary masterplanned communities operate through an economy of look-at-me iconography. On the urban scale, this leads to a bird's-eye image reduced to the simplicity of a comic strip: POW! However, this supersign is far from naive: the icon *doubles* Dubai's coastline and creates 78 kilometers of profitable waterfront property.[2] Furthermore, it acts as an organizational device: at street level, the plan of the palm tree creates a structure of control and an absence of choice.

To reform the refuge by engaging with the politics of iconography is to reconsider the long-range message and its close-up organizational qualities and consequences. How logo can one go? Superimposing the Palm's dead-end structure with a cross mark is one way of reformation from the air. At the level of the image, quickly captured and shared via Google Earth, the result updates a provocative statement: the Palm Jumeirah has checked out. Looking closer to the ground, the bold gesture can produce difference and urban complexity by connecting the formerly disjoined fronds. Here, canals act as cross streets while diagonal avenues fast-track travel times from the outer urban fringe to the suburban core.

Re:cover: From tabula rasa to integrated dynamic environment
Upscale retreats stand in the face of environmental forces in order to promote false conditions of constancy. The master cover-up is resource-intensive, illustrated by the momentous effort to mold Palm Jumeirah's breakwater, which includes seven million tons of rock, individually craned into place at the designated GPS coordinates. With grand designs on simulating a calm lagoon, the breakwater caused the stagnation of seawater and was subsequently modified with gaps to allow for the tidal oxygenation of the water.

Carrying this remedial measure further as a proactive strategy, a directional architecture emerges. By breaking the Palm at its narrowest points, thickening the foundations at its windward side, and giving over to the processes of erosion, the borough is both protected from and permeated by the water. The by-product of adapting to the natural currents is a setting enriched with different degrees of urbanity: canals that dissolve into a play of eddies, drifts, and wildlife.

Re:source I: From exhaustive fuels to solar geometry

The energy supply of this seemingly independent island relies on imports to fuel its cool artificial climate. This dislocation of decision-making and energy transportation dissociates urban form and architecture from its climatic context. Thus, any configuration attempting to turn four seasons into a steady springtime is made possible by environmental costs that are magically externalized. Air-conditioning bills on the Palm, however, expose the artifice, reaching up to €900 per month—a sum that underlines the disparaging limitations of the refuge.[3]

Urban layout can be a means to generate, save, and store energy on site. Reexamination of the existing urban structure exposes accidental but inherent geometries that reveal a bioclimatic opportunity. The curvilinear design of the Palm offers a readymade potential for electricity generation through solar concentration. The concave arrangement of "heliostat" power plants is adapted and installed onto the breakwater and fronds (including street surfaces and villa roofs) to create an array of flat mirrors that focus direct sunlight toward collectors situated at the pinnacle of the residential towers. Resource usage and urban layout now interlock. The proud solar towers become the new Burjs of Dubai, logically placed in terms of solar geometry and equally impressive in terms of high-rise living.

Re:source II: From representational to productive landscape

Today's exclusive retreats are dominated by representative sceneries dotted with highly consuming (palm) trees, but perhaps the prettiest place indeed is that of a fruitful garden, such as those found in the picturesque productive landscapes of Tuscany. In the case of Palm Jumeirah, the internal landscaping consists of large water surfaces designed to generate a picture-perfect location: one to purely view.

These optical surfaces afford opportunities for the redesign of metabolic flows. The niches are appropriated for agri- and aquaculture and modeled on the self-sustaining experiments of kibbutzim, in order to transform the representational landscape into a productive landscape, and provide enough nutrients and water for all borough inhabitants. Within the boundaries of the resort, fish, dates, citrus fruits, olives, and water can be harvested. Other agricultural goods such as eggs, dairy, cereals, and meats can be traded or purchased with the revenues from tourism procured from the only remaining hotel, the Atlantis. Internalizing the production of all necessary calories and water effaces transportation of a long-distance food system, narrowing the ecological footprint of the resort.[4]

With a quarter acre of productive landscape per person, the retrofitted Palm matches an updated version of Broadacre City,[5] which allotted one acre per family to promote a low-density urbanism. As a whole, the productive urban form is able to accommodate the flows of a semi-autotrophic metabolism.

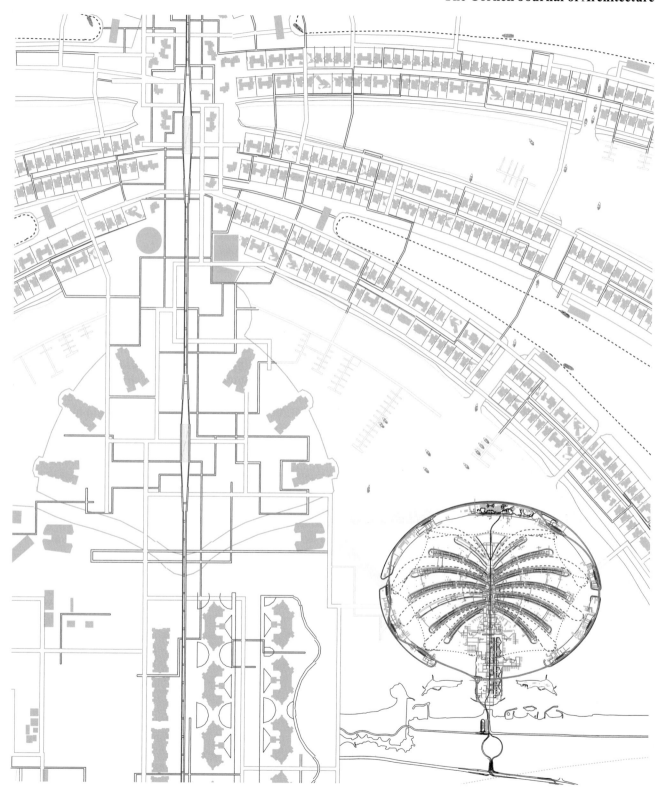

Re:block: From controlled checkpoints to a permeable grid

A typical enclave is based on a model of limited connectivity. First, accessibility is dominated by a single means—the individual car—as distances are too long and temperatures too hot to be covered on foot. Second, the circulation scheme is marked by limited entrances: a one-way toll road, or a stem that supports cul-de-sac branches. The treelike distribution system, literally inscribed onto the Palm's very figure, ultimately results in a highly controlled and limiting model of circulation.[6]

If the branches are regarded as a weave's warp then only the weft is missing in order to connect the fabric. With relatively minimal effort, a multidirectional city block can be grafted onto the Palm. Pedestrian networks (based on a maximum length of 200 m) thread through the lots to allow for waterfront accessibility. Boat-taxi routes are directed with the help of a few crossing canals, small bridges reach across points where the bays are narrow, and beach sands serve for camel or horse transportation.

The introduction of transverse links results in a multitude of continuous crossings, undetermined motion, and a choice of mode and way. After all, a city is not a tree, even less so a palm tree.[7]

Re:lock: From gates to go

A territorial retreat from society is organized by means of guarded barriers that lock strangers out of grounds. On the Palm, the subtle act of fortressing includes entry by a tolled highway (immediately excluding those not in possession of a car), an expensive monorail with only two operating stops, dead-end streets that discourage passersby, and significant entry fees and prices at various hospitality centers.

The infrared barricades develop into cornerstones for shading public buildings, their former security vacuums becoming converted civic parks and nature strips. Elevated highways are retained as shading devices, while access is organized via a web of smaller sinuous roads that pass through scattered meadows flourishing as a modern no-man's-land. Above, the monorail becomes mass transit as the number of stations is increased and the toll is reduced.

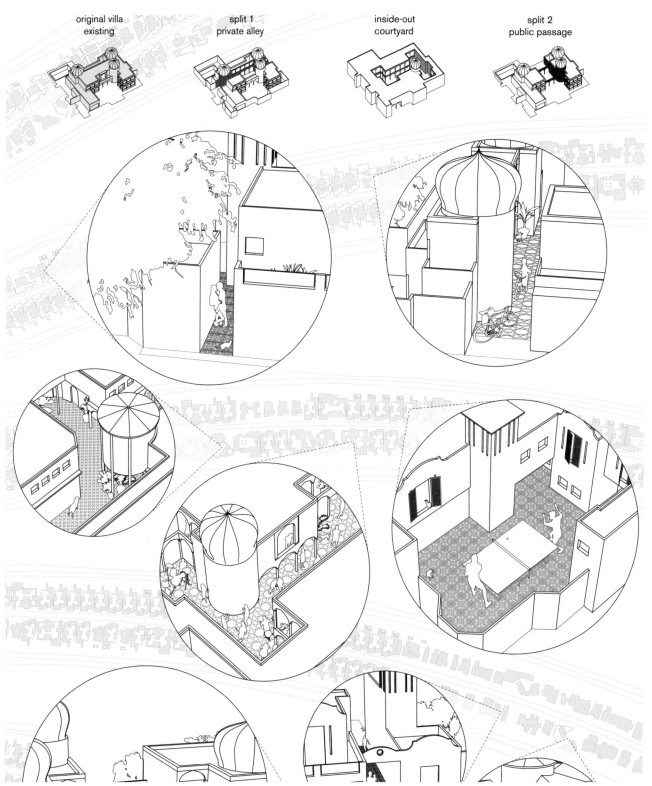

original villa
existing

split 1
private alley

inside-out
courtyard

split 2
public passage

Re: plot: From grand estates to affordable dwelling aggregates

Luxury refuges exclude on the basis of size and price. Villas on the Palm Jumeirah, ranging from 465 to 650 square meters, start selling at $2 million or are available for $15,000 per month, while those who built them earn a monthly average wage of $150.

Splitting villas and dividing plots is a means to obtaining smaller units (from 150 to 200 square meters) accessible to a broader range of inhabitants. It is the oversupply of equipment and generous circulation space of the estates that makes this operation possible: five-bathroom villas turn into five separate dwelling units; the "Central Rotunda," "Atrium Entry," and "Grand Foyer" styles offer smooth lines of division. The desirable side-effect of this measure is permeability at a pedestrian scale.

Re:use: From useless yards to inhabitable courtyards

Independent from geographic location, the design principles underlying luxury refuges are based on climate-controlled interiors while the outdoors remains exposed—a space for costly representation and buffering. Turning villas inside out results in courtyard typologies that provide shaded outdoor spaces suited to the climate. The extensive hardscaping surrounding the villas preempts its transformation into flooring while its perimeter marks the outline of new exterior walls. In reverse, interior marble floors turn into cool patio surfaces.

The civic consequence of this operation is a narrowing of the central access road. In the case of the Palm, the suburban tarmac is converted into an urban thoroughfare.

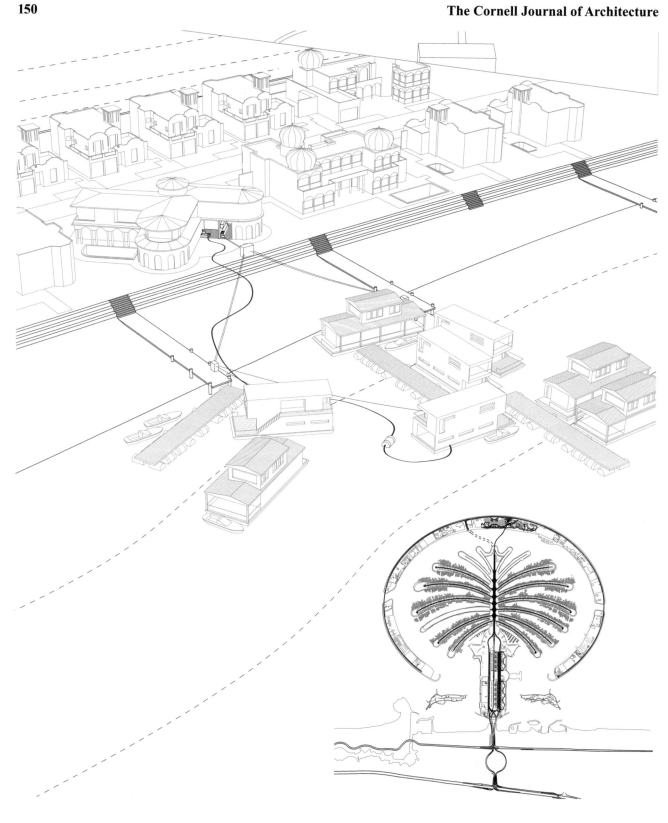

Re: View: From billboard architecture to local types
It is the horizontal view of the user that shapes the adapted refuge. Today's upscale refuges are based on a global catalog of marketable themes such as "Mediterranean," "Italian," "Santa Fe," or "Arabic," while offering the same Western typology, albeit in differing climatic or social contexts.

Combining the operations of splitting and reversal will deemphasize the themed decor in favor of a small-scale patio structure that develops different degrees of privacy. The Palm's 1,200-square-meters lots become mini-neighborhoods with public pathways, shared spaces, and private courtyards.

Re:gain: From property speculation to social appropriation
To create the ultimate location properties (waterfront and/or golf course access), luxury refuges embed a disproportionate amount of social capital, expertise, and labor. With the $10 billion and 40 thousand workers per day of construction,[8] all of Latin America's slums could have been equipped in one go.[9] A construction cost of $23 thousand per Palm-consumer translates to an upgrade of $665 per slum inhabitant.

Reconsidered in this way, Palm Jumeirah should provide the infrastructural framework to support 34 times as many people as it planned to. With the funds already spent, where would they dwell? Looking at the unused waterscape's ample voids, the Palm hints at an urban symbiosis of provision and supply, on the one hand, and self-organized extension, on the other hand. The voids can be regained and recuperated when needed: each residence provides facilities to a friend or relative on the water. Each frond supplies the fresh water, electricity, waste and transport lines to support an ad-hoc district following its own locally defined and negotiated rules.

The outcome is an urban fabric rigorously structured, yet open to modification at the same time. While making effective usage of the collective infrastructural investment, the borough leaves freedom for individual developments.

Ex-Palm is an application of the *Charter of Dubai,* exhibited within Refuge
at the International Architecture Biennale Rotterdam 2009. Collaborators:
Timothy Moore, Laura Saether, Tanner Clapham, Matthias Titze, Robert
Gorny, and Nathan Friedman. Research in cooperation with Berlin
University of Technology (Tutor: Andreas Quednau) and Stuttgart State
Academy of Art and Design (Tutor: Daniel Schönle).

Endnotes

1   Stephen Graham and Simon Marvin, *Splintering
    Urbanism: Networked Infrastructures, Technological
    Mobilities, and the Urban Condition* (New York:
    Routledge, 2001).

2   "At the start of the millennium, Dubai had become
    the fastest growing tourist destination in the world.
    This placed huge demands on its beaches and the
    idea was proposed to build a circular island offshore.
    HH Sheikh Mohammed Bin Rashid Al Maktoum
    then had the vision that an island in the shape
    of a palm leaf would maximize the beach area."
    "The Palm Story," Palm Jumeirah, Nakheel, website

    September 15, 2009 at http://www.palmjumeirah.
    ae/the-palm-story.php.

3   Robert Booth, "Pitfalls in Paradise: Why Palm
    Jumeirah Is Struggling to Live up to the Hype,"
    Guardian, April 26, 2008, website September 15,
    2009.

4   Brian Halweil and Thomas Prugh, *Home Grown:
    The Case for Local Food in a Global Market*
    (Danvers, MA: Worldwatch Institute, 2002).

5   Frank Lloyd Wright, *The Disappearing City*
    (New York: W.F. Payson, 1932).

6   Albert Pope terms this the path to urban closure,
    "'which always terminates in an exclusive destina-
    tion or end point' (Pope, 1996, 189)—the mall,

the suburban cul-de-sac, the fortified house garage"
(Stephen Graham and Simon Marvin, 2001).

7   "The units of which an artificial city is made up are
always organized to form a tree. So that we get a
really clear understanding of what this means, and
shall better see its implications, let us define a tree
once again. Whenever we have a tree structure, it
means that within this structure no piece of any unit
is ever connected to other units, except through the
medium of that unit as a whole. The enormity of this
restriction is difficult to grasp. It is a little as though
the members of a family were not free to make
friends outside the family, except when the family as
a whole made a friendship" (Christopher Alexander,
1965).

8   "Palm"-Eröffnung in Dubai: Mega-Show für
Superreiche, Spiegel website, November 21, 2008.

9   "Total investment required to upgrade slums,
by region, 2005–2020: Latin Americas and the
Caribbean: $9,6 bill. Slum upgrading would cost
$42 a year per beneficiary or $665 per beneficiary
over a period from 2005–2020. Estimates of the
investments required to upgrade slums include land
purchase and transfer, housing, network infrastructure, bulk infrastructure, schools and health clinics,
community facilities, planning and oversight,
community capacity building." Pietro Garau,
Elliott Sclar, and Gabriella Y. Carolini, *A Home in
the City* (London: United Nations Development
Programme, 2005).

FAKE Design cordially invites you to participate in **Ordos 100**, a collaborative architecture and design project in Inner Mongolia, China. We are inviting *you*, along with *100* architects from around the world to design *100* villas in less than *100* days per phase. There will be two phases from January-April, and May-August, 2008 in order to complete construction of the project within the year. For further information regarding the project description and detailed scheduling, please refer to the attached **file 1** and **file 2**.

FAKE Design will be responsible for curating the early stages of the design process, while ensuring quality control over the design concept and master planning, including all correspondence and coordination between the architects and client, Ordos Jiang Yuan Water Supply Co.

Also, please find attached a questionnaire regarding the assignment in **file 3**. Please confirm and send us a completed copy of the questionnaire before the **6th of January, 2008** deadline via email at: **ordos100@gmail.com**

Please be aware that all late entries will be disqualified.

This will be a rare and exciting opportunity for all eligible participants to come and collaborate with us in the New Year! We look forward to receiving your confirmation and meeting you soon!

Best Regards and Happy New Year,

Ordos Jiang Yuan Water Supplies Co.   Beijing FAKE Design Culture Development

Keller Easterling

is an architect and writer from New York City. She is the author of Enduring Innocence: Global Architecture and Its Political Masquerades *(MIT, 2005) and* Organization Space: Landscapes, Highways and Houses in America *(1999). A forthcoming book,* Extrastatecraft, *examines global infrastructure networks as a medium of polity.*

Pandas: A Rehearsal

The first invitation to join the ORDOS 100 went unanswered because a polite regret did not come to mind. The eager architect designing big villas in China has been, for me, the subject of some sport. A cheerful reminder that I had missed the deadline came as I was preparing a seminar about expanded repertoires of activism.[1] Assuming that righteous endgames might present activism's biggest restriction, the seminar looked past the symmetrical face-offs of resistance with their classic political pedigree to a dissensus that might be less self-congratulatory, less automatically oppositional, but more effective (and sneakier). Binary conflicts on battlegrounds, borders, and barricades shape our histories and habits of mind, sometimes lending them the very righteous violence we intend to dissipate. What would happen if one turned 90 degrees just before the finish line or kept pacing away from one's opponent in the duel, striding purposefully into a vast pasture of unorthodox techniques in situations not precast with enemies and innocents? In Milan Kundera's *The Joke,* when the prisoners are challenged to a race against the camp guards, they disarm the sprinting guards by running very slowly—by deploying a form of exaggerated compliance.

China's gift of two pandas (both named Unity) to Taiwan, was designed as a steamroller of sweetness and cuteness—the handshake as half nelson. The seminar naturally looked to stories like these and to a number of characters from pirates to princes to prisoners to comedians—Kundera, Michael K., Chauncey Gardiner, or Ai Weiwei—who successfully leverage power with slippery forms of dissent or misdirection. I realized that I might try to impress my students by deputizing myself as the seminar's own guinea pig, or panda, a pale academic panda, wandering into the very pastures in which we wished to rehearse. With their usual grace, the students allowed me my fiction, since one would have to be rather self-aggrandizing to find in this relatively benign situation enough controversy for an ethical struggle of any scale. Nor did they point out the cowardly insulation I enjoyed by being on a list with some of the world's most politically and culturally astute young architects.

Ai Weiwei's organization, FAKE, printed "Be Yourself" on the napkins at the Ordos Holiday Inn where the architects were sequestered for five days. The napkins and camera crews would suggest that 100 architects designing 100 villas were, like the 1001 Chinese workers in Ai Weiwei's Documenta project, players in a larger performance piece. While I support the idea of using architects as subjects in examinations of behavior, Ai Weiwei might have cast the wrong straw man. Surprisingly, the assumptions about what architects were and what they could do was not so hip. A project that most might regard as a revival of 20th-century international housing demonstrations, familiar suburbs, or 80s mannerism, Ai Weiwei seemed to regard as a thoroughly original exposé of architecture at the vanguard of new disciplinary habits. "From the start," the artist instructed, "this should be a star project, because in our human history, nobody has done anything like it. Architects are so educated, so concerned about protecting their knowledge, so attached to personal creativity rather than communicating and fighting and getting themselves into new circumstances and using their basic, original strength, their courage. Whenever you set up a condition questioning normal behavior, it's always interesting."[2] For Ai Weiwei, Ordos would be a stage for toying with the egos of architects and asserting himself as a better designer—one who had none of the attributes of the preening careerist or the turgid academic.

As the days went on in Ordos, the reminder that *we* had bitten on the hook and should be grateful for the chance to express ourselves was reinforced with shots of Mongolian moonshine and meals in a yurt-shaped Genghis Khan dinner theater. Fairy tales often accompany control. Power needs fictions and obfuscations that avoid any reckoning. One was forced to smile and nod in a situation constantly oscillating between acceptable and unacceptable conditions. Was the Paleo-Genghis new town of Ordos and its art neighborhood part of a macro-ecological experiment in preventing desertification, or was it another fortification of an autonomous region? Did it really mean something in this context to be allowed to be oneself? Was it not important simply to be part of an international network of colleagues? Should one *refuse* to work as if one's own soul or nation was somehow more pure? Was Ai Weiwei, now an authority figure rather than a critic, delivering a version of the "pretend smile" against which he protested in his withdrawal from the Olympics? Do refusals and self-regard enjoy a closer relationship than they should?

Still, the number 100 seemed interesting as a multiplier. Unlike the 1001 workers in Kassel, maybe a sympathetic group of 100 architects could upset the choreography by multiplying some intention that would tip the laughably dated zoo of villas toward other experiments. Could we not all turn in the same house to critique the homogeneity of the surrounding new town, or alternatively spread some invisible programmatic contagion through the population of villas without losing our precious option to express ourselves with building envelope?

A conference room at the Ordos Holiday Inn had been set up as a U.N., of sorts, for the international congress of architects. When the idea of such an epidemic was broached in this gathering, the architects returned to default forms of togetherness—utopian manifestos or charters of consensus that deadened any potentially productive epidemic with monism or righteousness. Most of the sentiments of U.N. architects involved green innovations, which the EU architects characterized as a laughable form of contrition. The discussion was laced with a little competition between conflicting formal camps. All in all, it fell neatly into the trap that had been set for clichéd architects.

But two can play at the game of fairy tales and pretend smiles. The project I presented gambled with a cocktail of pandas, compliance, and comedy to create a special "gift" of praise. With exaggerated compliance, the project congratulates the organizers for having an idea they never had. It notes the genius of camouflaging a place for independent voices within a banal suburban development—one even further disguised as a 1980s anachronism. The project proposes a micro-institution posing as a villa, suited to an arid climate and wrapped up as a chirpy, adorable, arm-twisting Panda.

With the "Be Yourself" napkin pinned over my heart for the final presentation, I thanked everyone for this journey of self-discovery. I noted the genius of the client to request big villas: what a clever ruse to use the symbol of class and exclusivity to *protect* cultural diversity within domesticity. Equally artful was the request for a home entertainment center for the villa. "Home entertainment" must be code for art venues in an otherwise absurdly vacuous new town. Moreover, the villa was so big that it could serve as a micro-institution in an art colony with its own capacity for openings, shows, and parties (e.g., Black Mountain or Yaddo). (Enclaves are sometimes built to exclude and sometimes built to protect the thing that is excluded. I was already convinced that Ordos, with its museum and studio buildings, represented the latter case.) With further praise, the project hinted at the foresight of planning big villas in a desert *previously* fueled by coal! "Like the rare Mongolian Antelope who stores fat in unlikely places," the presentation bluffed, the villa's adaptation to an arid climate would thus be a much more important demonstration of new, highly politicized global fuel alignments. Like a magician's box, the project's concentric arrangement facilitated public-private separations and "trap doors" within the house while also creating insulating layers for experiments with passive heating and cooling. In a bait and switch, only sweetened by current criticism of China, the project also ladled on some enthusiasm for the Olympics. The villa wisely called for a swimming pool, and fortunately it was big enough for a 25-meter Olympic training pool within which a young athlete might train outside the state system. Since most of China's Olympic swimmers are girls, the presentation noted the feminist intentions of the organizers. Within the concentric layers, special boxes, all of equal size, then might house guests and workers or artists and athletes in residence. Finally the presentation praised the owners of these villas, who were cool enough to want to share their house, not just to "be themselves" but also to "alter themselves."

The project is, like any project with impure thoughts, messy and partly wrong, and its rehearsal of techniques is less important than tripping the lock on potentially paralyzing restrictions to activism when there is so much to do. These techniques were also intended for situations of much more controversy and consequence than Ordos. Still, a rehearsal can open a door. One can rehearse the addictive pleasure and relief of deploying political craft in the service of something other than careerism or righteous certainty. The repertoire is inclusive of, in league with, and in excess of withdrawal (which always remains a possibility). Every global player is trying to see what the world can be taken for. I thought I should extend my (pale, academic) hand in another arm-twisting handshake—to raise the stakes or leverage a chance to do more.

Endnotes

1   *Architecture and Activism,* Yale School of Architecture, Spring 2008.
2   Quoted by Alex Pasternak in "Dawn of a New Century: Ordos 100," http://review.redboxstudio.cn/?p=175.

Project Credits

Keller Easterling, Fred Scharmen, R. Gerard Pietrusko, Andy Lucia, Matt Lake, Vivian Chin.

Photo on previous page: James Elaine.

In conversation with Rem Koolhaas
on Oswald Mathias Ungers

Rem Koolhaas heads the work of OMA, founded in 1975, and AMO, its conceptual branch focused on exploring territories beyond architectural and urban concerns. He is a professor at Harvard University where he conducts the Project on the City.

Oswald Mathias Ungers was a German architect, architectural theorist, and educator. He served as chair of the Department of Architecture at Cornell University from 1969 to 1975 and produced a number of built, theoretical, and text-based works before his death in 2007.

OMA RE: OMU

Interview by Jeremy Alain Siegel, Melissa Constantine, Matt Eshleman, and Steven Zambrano Cascante

Hommage à OMU, Axonometric, 1967, for Posthumous Exhibition, Galerie Strecker, Berlin, 1967, by Rainer Jagals. Drawn by Rainer Jagals, a 27-year-old student of Ungers, in the last year of his life, the abstract *Hommage à OMU* embodies a number of architectural concepts central to the pedagogy of O.M. Ungers, including typological transformation, metamorphosis, and "Variety in Unity." From the exhibition catalog: *Rainer Jagals,* Galerie Strecker, Berlin, 1967.

Jeremy

As you know, we are developing issue eight of the *Cornell Journal of Architecture*, which is titled *RE*. Our aim in this is to call attention to the conversation, the response, the back-and-forth, as a means of providing a location for meaningful dialogue. For you, design seems to be something treated less topically, but actually as a form of research and criticism, so we are happy that you have agreed to have this conversation with us on the subject of your early teacher and a major figure at Cornell, O.M. Ungers. I'd like to emphasize that this should be seen as our attempt, as students, to understand our current moment and future trajectory *through* this history that we are only familiar with secondhand, so we will focus on certain resonances between the two careers—that of Ungers, and your own—with the aim of explicating both histories. I'd like to begin with the biographical moment just prior to your discovery of Ungers, at the Architectural Association in London. What was the initial attraction for you to Ungers, to the United States, and to Cornell?

Rem

It would have been 69 or 70 when I first came into contact with Ungers' work in Berlin. I was a student at the AA doing my thesis on the Berlin Wall as architecture. It was in Berlin that I discovered the pamphlets that Ungers was producing, which I found incredibly exciting because at the AA there was simply no sympathy for interests in formal issues. But in these pamphlets

Architecture 1966–1969, TU Berlin. O.M. Ungers with Guido Ast, Heidede Becker, Claas Corte, Uwe Evers, Ulrich Flemming, Stephen Katz, Henner Oppermann, Horst Reichert, and Volker Sayn. Images courtesy of the Technical University of Berlin.

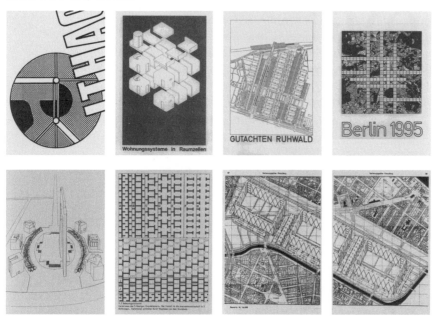

it was there in abundance. So my main attraction to America at that point was Ungers. But at the same time I was vaguely aware that I wanted to do something on the subject of New York City. I also knew that I wanted to take a more indirect movement toward the city in order to have a better sense of America before I actually got to New York, so the presence of Ungers was an added incentive to begin at Cornell.

Jeremy

What did it mean to come here to study America, when both Ungers and Colin Rowe spent a good deal of their energy studying Europe?

Rem

In the 70s, I think the interaction between America and Europe was much less fraught than it is now, and far more spontaneous. Particularly in the art world—Joseph Beuys was here, Andy Warhol was there—so there was really a perceptible symmetry, where both parties were enjoying each other's energy. And although when I first knew him he was working very hard on his return to Europe as a professional, America was still a very strong part of Ungers' interests, for instance in the projects he did on American communes.

Melissa
As you often defer to the language of popular culture, politics, or statistics to describe the city, how would you characterize your approach with respect to Ungers, for whom analysis was carried out in almost purely architectural terms?

Rem
I think that what is almost impossible for somebody who has not experienced it to understand is really what the *essence* of Ungers was. It was not a way of thinking or any kind of method, but an unbelievably exhilarating presentation of his own way of thinking. It was almost an ecstasy on his part, and in this ecstasy you would be made constantly aware of how a small beginning could be manipulated through an endless series of variations, transformations, or new ideas projected onto it. It was really about being in the presence of a virtuoso of thinking—or even a virtuoso of intuition—perhaps *intuition* is a better word than *thinking* in his case.

Photograph, 1971. From left: Werner Seligmann, Unknown, Fred Koetter, O.M. Ungers, Jerry Wells. Image courtesy of Arthur Ovaska and the Cornell AAP Archives.

So more than being about a contrast between one way of looking at the city and another, it was really about the fact that you could be so intuitive about the city itself and the fact that we were sharing so many of these intuitions. Being together actually forced us to go further in what each was doing, as a kind of shared operation. I think this intense communication was really the whole value of the thing; in a way architectural issues were partly on the side. The other important thing to realize about the time is that although there were of course many archives at Cornell, many rare book collections, map collections, and so on, information about New York City was actually quite sketchy. So it was not necessarily a divergence between Ungers, who was really interested in looking at architectural issues, and me, who wanted to extend this "looking" into popular culture, but it was more that you had to look at popular culture in order to understand these specific phenomena, and to the extent that I shared our discoveries with Mathias, it was something he seemed to be interested in as well.

Matt

You have said that it is your ambition to practice architecture as a journalist. And even during your time as a journalist at *De Haagse Post*, which preceded your entry into architecture, you practiced an extreme form of journalism— abstention from "moralization or interpretation of real phenomena," and instead "the intensification of reality; starting point: an uncompromising acceptance of reality."

Rem

Ironically that's what journalism was back then. It was not really extreme. "New Journalism" was largely an American invention. I was working for a newspaper that was acting as a workplace for almost a whole section of the Dutch literary avant-garde. It was a particular culture that was really related to Fluxus, an art movement that was interested in looking at facts, and rarely at glamour. Mathias was also a friend of many artists, so there was that affinity. But at that time, this objectivity was an inevitable phenomenon and not a form of radicality.

Melissa

There is a resonance between your ambition to practice architecture as a journalist, and Ungers' interest in addressing reality, which of course is also echoed in the idea of the paranoiac, as you describe in *Delirious New York*.

Rem

It may be incredibly difficult to imagine, currently, how *un-pompous* culture was then. Right now many people have a sense that they have a position, a position to maintain, and that the result is an increased formalism in interactions. So perhaps it is not dialogue that is disappearing, but spontaneity that has really been drained from interaction. There are many reasons for this: it has to do with email and other phenomena, but basically at that time people didn't take themselves seriously. And this was not just true for Ungers, who was interested in everything, but for example, Michel Foucault was in Ithaca, and we would go picnicking. I cannot claim any kind of significant intellectual influence of course, because I only picnicked—but in many ways this kind of informality was everywhere, and it was just fun. Architecture was a small part of it, and probably an important part, and at certain moments a really dominating part, but it was really a seamless intellectual and nonintellectual situation. The absence of that in current academic and cultural situations is very noticeable.

Melissa

How did this situation play out in the relationship between Rowe and Ungers?

Rem

I should say that at that time Ungers was very tortured because he had to deal with a traumatic situation in which the person who invited him repudiated him the moment he arrived. That was real torture. He was somebody who was fundamentally so sensitive that this had made him extremely insecure. In his insecurity he looked for many different versions of and possibilities for architecture. It might be something that is hard to appreciate now, but it was very significant that I, as a Dutchman, befriended a German. Even in 72 that was a big deal. Germans were used to hostility; a kind of blanket hostility. Even in the context of Team X, which was very important for Mathias, he was never quite taken seriously. He was just tolerated, and in fact they would always whisper anti-Teutonic grumblings, and there was always an awful undercurrent of skepticism toward Germans, which I didn't have any of. Actually, I had quite an opposite, almost recalcitrant attitude toward the skepticism.

Jeremy
We have a clipping from the *Cornell Daily Sun*, a letter to the editor which was titled "Formalist Pigs"—and you signed it. It really captures the intensity of this conflict.

Rem
I think that between Rowe and Ungers—and this is why I brought up the German thing—it really was about this allergy of the Anglo-Saxon temperament that could not deal with the energy and emotionalism with which Mathias would mobilize his argument.

Formalist Pigs. Letter to the Editor, *Cornell Daily Sun*, February 19, 1973, by Chas Alexander, Peter Allison, Gerardo Brown, Werner Goehner, Paul Hollenbeck, Rem Koolhaas, Ed Russel, Diego Suarez, and Larry Harmon. Image Courtesy of the *Cornell Daily Sun* and Werner Goehner.

Formalist Pigs

Letters to the Editor

To the Editor:

Any outsider with sufficient interest to follow the reports, editorials and letters concerning recent events in the department of architecture and published in The Sun would, in our opinion, be left with a garbled and grossly unfair

impression of the actual situation. He would have been treated to the ghastly scene of three innocent

formalists mistakenly sacrificed to yesterday's gods, science and technology; he would have heard

several outspoken professors and a great many students so overcome by disgust at such conspicuous waste as

to be incapable of pursuing their work; and eventually he would have understood that in this vacuum of

irresponsibility only one man could possibly be to blame. This is the stuff of Paranoia.

In contrast, our experience is far less stimulating. We accept the contract and tenure decisions as a legitimate and inevitable aspect of policy planning. We see the unsuccessful attempt to mobilize student opposition to the decisions as an act of selfrighteous cynicism. And the current campaign to vilify Architecture Chairman Oswald M. Ungers while threatening total disruption to the department would seem to establish an absolute low in bad taste and irresponsibility.

There is indeed a group of 'formalist pigs' (Prof. Werner Seligmann's phrase) struggling desperately to retain their sphere of influence within the department. In their position evidently any mean trick is worth pulling, even if only to contribute to the general confusion.

In the face of continual provocation and much abuse, the chairman has, in our opinion, continued to exercise his responsibilities with great restraint and complete integrity. We deeply resent the suggestion that due to his activity the department is in chaos and all work at a standstill. This is no more then wishful thinking on the part of a minority who seem intent on holding the department to ransom as the only means of protecting their

careers.
Chas Alexander grad
Peter Allison grad
Gerardo Brown grad
Larry Doll grad
Werner Goehner grad
Paul Hollenbeck grad
Rem Koolhaas grad
Ed Russel grad
Diego Suarez grad
Larry Harmon grad
Students in the department of architecture.

Jeremy

In looking at the works that epitomized the opposition between Rowe and Ungers, we could say that the answer to Rowe's Collage City would have been Ungers' Green Archipelago. Have these two understandings of the city impacted your understanding of the contemporary city in any way?

Rem

I think it is very difficult to appreciate how surprisingly ideology-free America was in 72, particularly American architectural education. Coming from a post-May 68 Europe that was completely obsessed with ideology, it was astonishing to see a figure like Colin Rowe, who really seemed to be like a kind of surgeon who had taken out entire sections of the collective American brain, and made sure that they would never again be able to think about ideology and only ever about form. And he was clearly doing it in a very efficient way, so that there were whole generations of American architects who, no matter how smart, were actually contemptuous of architecture as a social thing. He really succeeded in making the social the height of absurdity. So I always found *Collage City* interesting as a series of manipulations, but at the same time I was really allergic to the aesthetic it advocated, because I think that the essence of Colin Rowe is that he liked the aesthetics of historical accident but not the conditions that cause accident. In other words, he liked traces of a disaster or collision, but simply as an aesthetic, and not as evidence of a confrontation. So, in terms of my understanding of the city, I don't think that *Collage City* had any particular impact, except perhaps in making me utterly skeptical of any architect's thinking of the city. This was very different with Mathias exactly because we had some of the same experiences in common. Even though he was older, and had experienced the war firsthand, we had both experienced the postwar situation, when being in the ruined city was a typical thing. Rotterdam, and even Amsterdam in certain sections, was completely ruined. So for both of us, it was extremely easy to imagine not only a ruined European city, but the instability of and actual removal of significant parts.

Die-Stadt-in-der-Stadt (Cities-Within-the-City, or The Green Archipelago). Axonometric, 1977, by O.M. Ungers, Hans Kolhoff, Rem Koolhaas, Arthur Ovaska, and Peter Riemann. Berlin as archipelago. Image Courtesy of Arthur Ovaska and the Cornell AAP Archives.

Ville Nouvelle Melun-Senart. Proposal to the City of Lille, 1987, by Rem Koolhaas, Yves Brunier, Xaveer de Geyter, Mike Guyer, and Luc Reuse. French suburbia as archipelago. Image courtesy of OMA.

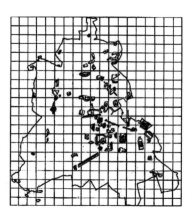

Die-Stadt-in-der-Stadt. Detail, 1977, by Peter Riemann.
Image courtesy of Arthur Ovaska and the Cornell AAP
Archives.

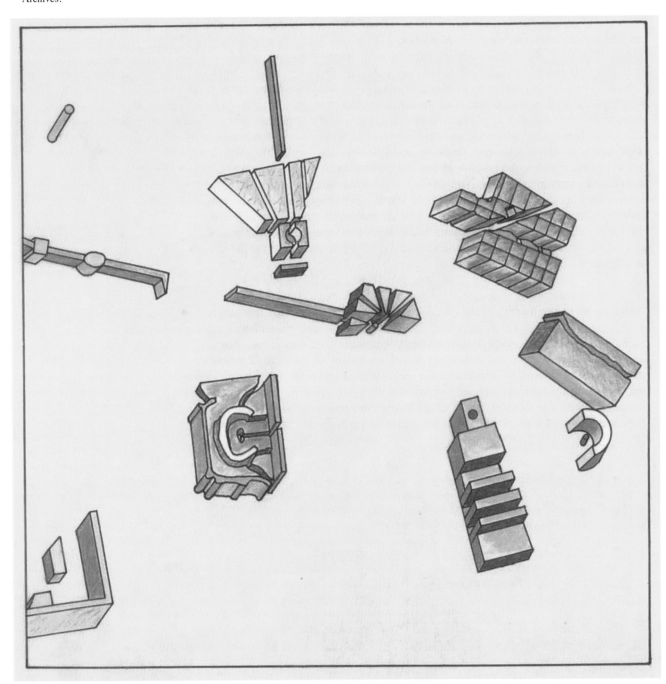

By the time we did the Green Archipelago in 77, Rotterdam had been rebuilt, Amsterdam had been restored, but Berlin, because of its East-West division, was still a city where the traces of the war were incredibly strong and where you could even say there was a unique aesthetic that was based as much on the presence as on the absence of certain things. And we both liked that, perhaps not for quite the same reasons, but the aesthetics of it were overwhelmingly attractive, and I think that from that point to a campaign of removal was actually a very small step. So in a certain way it may seem like a radical thing, but what we were actually saying was, "let's just adopt the landscape of 15 years ago."

Jeremy

This relates to your more recent focus on the contemporary city, that is, the preserved city. We see this in your proposal for Milstein Hall, but also OMA has put a significant amount of attention into this in its work on Beijing and in the Hermitage project, for example. And while one can often point to the "sustain-able" project to explain the interest in preservation, I think that for you it is about something else. Can you situate your interest in preservation within your concerns as a journalist, and how this might relate to Ungers' fascination with the existing situation as such?

Rem

Are there actually any projects of preservation by Ungers, apart from the Green Archipelago? I'm trying to think why it didn't extend to actual preservation at some point. Perhaps the advantage of having been a journalist, rather than someone with a journalistic curiosity or an interest in real situations, is that a journalist actually puts himself in situations of ignorance and rectifies that ignorance. When you start to do something about somebody and you know nothing about them, you start reading, you meet them, and then you know something about them. I think the difference between Ungers and myself is that he would never put himself in these situations

Rem Koolhaas conducting interview with ex-Mayor of New York John Lindsay.

and that I was actually used to putting myself in them. That, in the end, was a huge advantage for me, in the sense that first of all, I can admit ignorance, but that I also know the procedures to undo ignorance. I think that was really the whole difference between what he was doing here and what I was doing at Harvard with the *Project on the City*, where we simply said, "I know nothing about this, you know nothing about this: let's try to find something out." That was based on intuitions, of course, but these versions of ignorance were actually important errors that ultimately had crucial things to contribute to an understanding of architecture. I have to admit that when we started preservation, it really felt like a completely crazy world; as if it had nothing to do with us, no possible connections. But when we started to look, we realized that actually it was a significant part of modernity. So it's really about a kind of professional attitude toward the undoing of ignorance.

Steven
Within the informal city, an example of which you have been looking at in Nigeria with the *Project on the City*, we begin to see localized difference coalescing into larger systems from the bottom up. In Lagos, however, your interpretation has focused on the larger systems of Western infrastructure within which these processes unfold. How does Ungers' idea of the accommodation of difference within larger systems differ with respect to what you have learned from Lagos?

Rem
My interest in Lagos was born of a moment set by my own enthusiasm for and confidence in the act of planning, at a time when even the whole idea that the city could be influenced was at a very low point. It was also maybe the first moment where we could sense that the contemporary city was something fundamentally different and uncontrollable, and therefore needed to be rethought completely because the existing architectural repertoire was no longer relevant. I started, in the spirit that you mentioned, to think of Lagos as a self-organizing system, but in the end I was able to reveal some of the radical steps of planning that had actually established a framework for that self-organization. So, what started as an effort to really plumb the depths of skepticism, in the end, ten years later, had become a position somewhere between total pessimism and, still, the discovery that *some* planning had gone into it, and that this planning could explain the outcome of the situation. Now that Lagos is actually in much better shape, you can see that this formal aspect of the city is reemerging and the city is becoming more conventional and less self-organized. So I think that self-organization was, in a way, an aspect of a crisis rather than a fundamental part of the whole thing.

Steven
There is also a difference in the kind of system that you and Ungers seem to be interested in. For Ungers' interests in physical systems—infrastructural and territorial scale projects, typological systems, unit agglomerations—there is your focus on what might be thought of as organizational or political systems—in your work with the European Union for example, or the three-part series on power done for *Volume* magazine. What are the implications for the role and function of the building within the larger system in each case?

Rem

When Mathias came back from America, I think he did a number of projects that were really radical, and that in my view, introduced a new way of doing buildings, and a new way of thinking about the relationship between idealism and the real. For instance, the big Messe-Torhaus in Frankfurt is a part of this engagement in very circumstantial and very bizarre situations. And of course there came this other period in his life where seemingly he completely closed off any connection with that past and only did perfect shapes in relatively perfect conditions.

Messe-Torhaus, Frankfurt-am-Main. Perspective, 1983–1984, by Buro O.M. Ungers. Image courtesy of Edition Lidiarte.

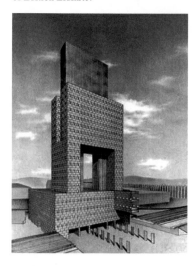

I've never taken that position very seriously, because I always was able to think, "that's not really him," but clearly it was totally him and he was wholly invested in it and took it very seriously. I kept thinking that it was just a phase, because Ungers was in a very important way a person of phases. I would say that perhaps one of the big differences between his work and our work is that, although ours looks very different, maybe you can really explain it as a very boring line of development, much more than his work, which is radically different at different times of his life.

Melissa

Along those lines, can you speak about the design and development of Milstein Hall with respect to this more typological evolution within the office?

Rem

If you look at our work in America, and if you look at the basic incentive of looking at America, it was of course not to study New York, it was fundamentally to understand how architecture has changed. Both *Delirious New York* and also the *Harvard Guide to Shopping* ask: What is the effect of steel? What is the effect of air conditioning? What is the effect of multiplication? In that effort, there is a very puritanical hope that style and even form can be transcended and superseded, and for everyone remotely interested in that direction, there is the box.

23 East 22nd Street. From lecture, "Stress Test,"
Cornell University, 2010 by Rem Koolhaas. The stepped
box as an American phenomenon. Image courtesy
of OMA.

Paul Milstein Hall. Construction, May, 2010.
Photograph by William Staffield. Image courtesy
of Cornell AAP.

Paul Milstein Hall. "Ungers-like paradoxes."
Milstein Hall as sectional building. Image courtesy
of OMA.

The box is a very important part of our work—Milstein is one of many—and I think that, in retrospect, that is what America taught us. America gave us the tools to extend the illusion that you could go beyond form for a very long time. Then there is the further pleasure of showing that the box can be incredibly contextual, that the box is not necessarily a stand-alone, but on the contrary can be the connection between a number of different worlds; that a box can have a section, et cetera. So in that sense you could say that in the case of Milstein there are a series of Ungers-like paradoxes that are projected onto the box.

Jeremy

This relates to our discussion about approaches to difference. You've said that a course on wines was the most valuable you took at Cornell; wine also seems to be an apt metaphor for architecture—there is typology, or species, there is site, or terroir, variation across locale, a desired end form. Ungers, too, was interested in the accommodation of difference, but in difference that was always contained within a certain consistency of language, i.e., "variety in unity." OMA's work is, on the one hand, interested in that, as in its interest in the box, but at the same time it is interested at times in the emergence of certain formal and material languages. The box itself is something you explain as an emergence from a specifically American context. Can you talk about your divergence from Ungers in this respect?

Rem

I'm not a materialist, but I think that maybe the 18-year difference in age between Mathias and I really explains everything for me, because it was just the kind of difference between the possibility of being a humanist and not being a humanist. From that there is a whole chain of consequences. Mathias could still believe that he was part of a tradition, part of a line, and a whole genealogy of relationships. Even though I am also related, I am part of many lines, this 18 years makes all the difference in terms of what your *world* is. At that time Europe and America were the world. The non-West existed, of course, but it was not a particularly compelling or urgent part of our considerations. Now we ourselves are becoming almost secondary and the action is somewhere else and that means a radically different relationship with language and place. That tiny shift of barely even a generation is enough to explain vast differences.

Jeremy

Postmodernity or globalization as the kind of hinge …

Rem

I would say so, yes. And also of course the plethora of other cultures that then become relevant in your work. I don't think that at any point anything non-Western was important for Mathias. In Mathias's time, you could have a particular body of education that took you from the beginning to the end. I think that is now much more fragile because you literally have to learn all other cultures and all other languages, all the time. This alone creates an instability.

Melissa

To return to the reading of Milstein as a box and as a connector, you are saying something through this project about how our college will function. What do you envision for the future of architectural education and in what trajectory do you see it heading?

Rem

Initially we were interested in using a box as a place where very specific things could be organized, which is also not a typical way of looking at a box; there was a library, there were very particular subdivisions ... But if you look at the development of the project, I think more and more it has simply become a place of interaction and a place of work. That probably testifies to a situation where the stability of specificity in education has been abandoned in favor of process, more than formal organizations or predictable configurations. And that is the beauty of a box: that this kind of flux moment can at some point become rooted again.

Melissa

Do you think that this better accommodates the architect who will then be working in a globalized mode?

Rem

I'm not cynical about education, but when I was being educated myself, I was aware that you learn only so much in an education, but most of what you learn you learn from your context, you learn from the city or the environment that you are in, you learn from reading the paper. I think that education is certainly a kind of a freeze-frame that collects a number of well-meaning people in a well-meaning process, but whether it is actually equipping you to act in a certain way? I'm dubious.

Yehre Suh

is an architect and a visiting critic at Cornell University Department of Architecture. She is currently preparing an exhibition on Rowe and Ungers and their pedagogical production during the 1960 through 1970s at Cornell University.

Rowe × Ungers: Untold Collaborations

As a visitor to Cornell University, Department of Architecture, one cannot escape the mysticism and folklore surrounding the stories of Colin Rowe and Oswald Mathias Ungers during their period of cohabitation on this remote plateau of academic bliss. The ghosts of the two figures lurk behind every corner and every encounter. The extraordinary stories of personal escapades and incidental conflicts are relished as part of the school's legacy and continue to hold ground as part of institutional history. What exactly happened during this period of coexistence to have produced such productive influential work persists as an irresistible project of pedagogical archeology.

Latent collaboration and competition marked the period when Rowe and Ungers both taught at Cornell. Due to bureaucratic situations and institutional grievances, the relationship has not been recorded as being mutually profitable. But the state of confusion in which architecture existed in this tumultuous period—not dissimilar to the discipline's current cacophony—allowed for a common aspiration and rigor in promoting a theory of architecture that envisioned new methodologies and modes of thought. Despite the infamous stories of conflict, it is more important to note their mutual understandings of critical conditions for architecture, and the urgency to establish new grounds for speculative productions.

A comparative understanding of their work is significant for us today for several reasons. Theoretical armatures were constructed through the disciplinary languages of architecture as a means for exploring a mode of operation resistant to, yet critical of the political, social, economic, and cultural turmoil of the period. To project beyond the reclusive banality of the picturesque and sci-fi utopianism, they sought a disciplinary autonomy that would actively engage, not ignore, society in the conceptualization of architectural languages throughout the city. Their methodologies were based on extensive research and analysis, processed through iterative adjustments of pedagogical frameworks. Studio and thesis projects became laboratories of larger experiments and publications and exhibitions were utilized as tools of analytical production. Crucially, architecture and the city were understood as flexible systems in constant flux. Rowe and Ungers shared the aspiration for an alternative path between the ideological resistance of the existing city and the authoritarian trauma of modern planning. Urban strategies were deployed as malleable mechanisms in which object and field were in continuous dialogue and as network systems that accommodated the inevitable changes and transformations of urban conditions.

Take, for example, Rowe's proposal for Harlem in Upper Manhattan in the
New City: Architecture and Urban Renewal Exhibition at MoMA, New York,

and Ungers' proposal for the area between 32nd Street and 42nd Street in the *Urban Block* and *Gotham City: Metaphors & Metamorphosis*.

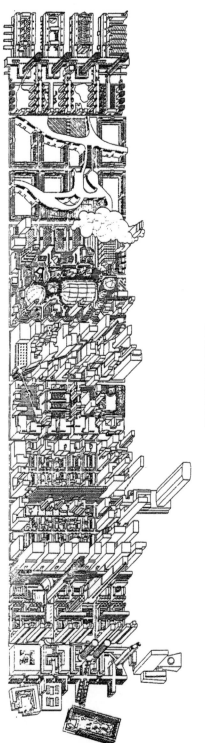

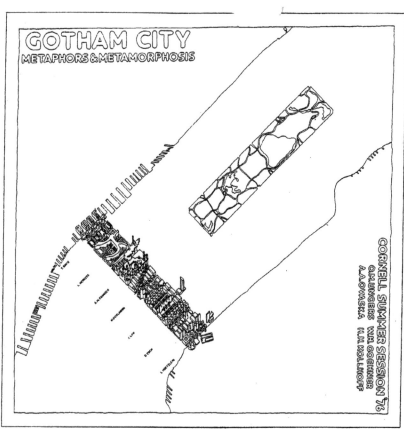

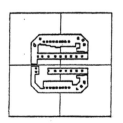

The two projects, executed in 1967 and 1976 respectively, utilized Manhattan as a site to test the latest theories on the identity of architecture and the city. Although the projects are almost a decade apart, both works were an attempt to address the overt anxieties of new development and construction against the urgency of the imminent disappearance of the existing city. In the 1960s, Manhattan was experiencing the biggest construction boom since the 1930s. Massive redevelopment was accompanied by large-scale destruction. It was a period of internal conflict in which new megadevelopments were being realized alongside discussions regarding the history, architectural heritage, and preservation of the existing city fabric. In 1961, the new zoning law took effect, which encouraged an "open" city idea, reminiscent of Le Corbusier's Plan Voisin of 1925. The Late Modernism of the 1950s was being amended by Historicist Modernism, exemplified in projects such as Philip Johnson's New York State Theater at Lincoln Center in 1964, Edward Durell Stone's Gallery of Modern Art in 1964, and Minoru Yamasaki's World Trade Center Towers in 1973. Meanwhile, at the other end of the spectrum, Jane Jacobs' *The Death and Life of Great American Cities* was published 1961, and with the establishment of the Landmarks Preservation Commission in 1965 and the gradual waning of the legacy of Robert Moses, preservation of the traditional scale and character of city street life became an essential part of the discourse surrounding architecture and city planning. In this context, Rowe's *Collage City* and Ungers' *Cities Within the City* became projective manifestos to test and investigate the new directions in architecture and city that were critical of the disciplinary anxiety of the times and proposed an urban vision for the new collective. This is what remains pertinent to us now.

If the decades of the 1960s and 1970s are recognized as a period when Modernist ideals were questioned and the profession was infused with self-doubt, we find ourselves in a similar situation today, as the practice struggles to identify its position within the multiplicity of aphasic spectacles and the discord of heterogeneous complacencies. In this sense the critical modus operandi of Rowe × Ungers can be regarded as a tool for reengaging and critiquing the discipline in its current state. To know what is to be, we need to know what was before.

See Rowe × Ungers timeline at cornelljournalofarchitecture.cornell.edu.

Credits

All images courtesy of the MIT Press and the O.M. Ungers Archive. Colin Rowe and Fred Koetter, *Collage City*, ©MIT 1995, by permission of the MIT Press. Colin Rowe, edited by Alexander Caragonne, *As I Was Saying, Volume 3: Urbanistics*, ©MIT 1978, by permission of The MIT Press.

Kent Kleinman

Kent Kleinman is the Gale and Ira Drukier Dean of Cornell University's College of Architecture, Art, and Planning. His scholarly focus is 20th-century European Modernism, and his publications include Villa Müller: A Work of Adolf Loos; Rudolf Arnheim: Revealing Vision; Mies van der Rohe: The Krefeld Villas; *and a translation of Jan Turnovsky's* The Poetics of a Wall Projection.

RE: Architecture or Design: Wither the Discipline?

May 21, 2010

Dear Peter,

Gauntlets thrown are hard to ignore when they come emblazoned with a caption. You recently gave a lecture here at Cornell with the title "Architecture or Design: Wither the Discipline?" The lecture was a direct response to my initiative to expand the boundary conditions of the domains encompassed by this college, and I cannot but accept the invitation to reply.

Defending the borders of a discipline is, it seems to me, not that different from defending borders more generally, and inevitably risks becoming an essentialist exercise. I have doubts that it is possible to circumscribe a field that has such a voracious demand for imported goods and services. But more to the point, I have doubts that the project is worth the effort, for the porosity of the border is, I believe, not a weakness that needs strengthening but rather a desirable weakness, a weakness that allows it to endure. I write to you, however, not to convince you that yours is a difficult task, but for a more tactical reason: to provoke you to expand on your position that it is useful and possible to draw a solid line around the field, to describe, with any operational precision, an "inside." If you succeed, I learn.

I have, as you know, moved in the opposite direction, and argued instead for the pleasure and utility of a sprawling, unruly, sometimes ill-behaved, often opportunistic activity that claims as its intellectual and practical domain the shape and the shaping of the built environment. I have further claimed that Cornell's College of Architecture, Art, and Planning might do well to consider this domain its particular responsibility and territory. And I have given this activity a name—design—and believe, of course, that the field of architecture will not wither but flourish under this identity and expand creatively under less carefully policed borders.

I am not arguing that the making and theorizing of, say, shoes, is identical to the making and theorizing of buildings, although even such classically trained disciplinarians as Erwin Panofsky saw plenty of connections between Gothic shoes, Gothic architecture, and scholastic literary form, and he is certainly not alone in cross-fertilizing genres. I am also entirely committed to the project of subject expertise, even though expertise is a rather conservative concept based largely on pre-existing knowledge domains (that is, expertise is pre-authorized, vetted, and sanctioned by peers and experience). I would not, however, want to define architecture as the sum of its past knowledge, as the aggregate of its expertise, and I would not like to exclude the Panofskys from the pantheon of architectural thinkers. I subscribe to an architecture that embraces an expansive space of speculation undergirded by subject expertise, and one of the principle means of traversing this domain is through intentional acts of design.

Design was once understood as the differentiator between the natural and the artificial. Borrowing the language (and insights) of Bruno Latour, design differentiates between matters of fact and matter of concern. Following this distinction, nature is a found condition, given, uncontested, subject to description but not critique. The constructed world, on the other hand, is fundamentally normative, defined in deontic terms. What Latour has recently argued, what the entire "cyborg" culture (Donna Haraway et al.) has long proclaimed, and what I find very appropriate for architects to ponder, is that the increasing, almost ubiquitous use of the term "design" coincides with an expanding recognition that, in the end, there are really only matters of concern. The construction of the artificial has expanded to a point where it is no longer intellectually viable to argue for the nature/artifact binary. Latour's endgame, clearly articulated in a keynote address of 2008 titled "A Cautious Prometheus," was to show that we have arrived at a moment where even the climate is discussed, quite publically, as a designed condition; the entire global climate change debate is predicated on the presupposition that the climate is a matter of fact no longer. If you accept this, then there is, quite literally, no outside, no border. All is design.

Perhaps "all is architecture" would be more appealing to you, but I do not think so, for your project has always been to explore the machinery of architecture, and not the grist that goes in or the meal that comes out. To sustain a disciplinary interior, you need to uphold the essential distinction between the millstone and the grain. I contend that precisely this distinction has blurred to the point of irrelevance.

I hope, Peter, to hear back from you soon.

Your good friend,

Kent Kleinman
Gale and Ira Drukier Dean

Peter Eisenman

is a Cornell graduate, an internationally recognized architect and the Charles Gwathmey Professor of Architecture at Yale. His award-winning projects include the Memorial to the Murdered Jews of Europe in Berlin, the Wexner Center for the Visual Arts at the Ohio State University, and the Koizumi Sangyo Corporation headquarters in Tokyo.

RE: RE: Architecture or Design: Wither the Discipline?

Author's Note: This text was written for the *Cornell Journal of Architecture*. It derives from a lecture of the same title given at Cornell in March of 2010. It was originally intended to suggest why the term *architecture* should remain central in the name of the College, rather than, as has been suggested, changing the name of the school to the College of Design. This text is written as a resistance to not only the culture of commodification, but also the entrance of that culture into the university in a not too surreptitious manner.

Today, design is a goal-oriented practice which through aesthetic and economic means attempts to seduce mass culture into ever increasing consumption (one example: the iPhone). In this sense, design has become a unique, omnipresent, synthetic activity; it encompasses everything. This was not always the case. Sometime in the 16th century the Italian terms *disegno* and *colore* came to signify a dialectical pair used to describe the typological differences between Florentine (*disegno*) and Venetian (*colore*) painting. But *disegno* was also, and importantly, dialectical. *Disegno* was thought to be work that began with the drawing of an outline or the form of a figure, while *colore* was meant to suggest the importance of color, which took whatever form it needed without any a priori formal content or contour. *Disegno*, from the very beginning, was seen to be more rational and conceptual, while *colore* was seen as more emotional and expressionistic. The activity of *disegno* always had an a priori objective; that is, the maintenance in the work of the original formal outline, the prepainting or cartoon to which the final aspired. In its most generic sense, *disegno* was the proper relationship of parts to a whole.

Thus, *disegno* was not painting itself but a subset or tendency of painting. It was only later in the 16th century, with Vasari's idea of *Arti del Disegno* (literally, the arts of design), that design became a comprehensive discipline, and painting a function of it. That is, the idea of design shifted from a dialectical and analytic category to a synthetic one, to a totalizing attitude, one which contained the seeds of the design activity that is ubiquitous in the present.

At the same time that *disegno* became an operative term, so too did architecture. Architecture as a named discipline did not exist before the 16th century. Prior to that, it was seen simply as building and construction mediated by a transcendental will. This all changed with Brunelleschi and Alberti and their work with perspective, which established the human subject and the eye of that subject as the mediator between the architectural object and the subject. This mediation shifted the notion of a transcendent mediation or metaphysic to an immanent one. It was now no longer sufficient to assume that the Vitruvian triad of commodity, firmness, and delight constituted architecture; rather, as Alberti writes in *De Re Aedificatoria*, a structure no longer merely held something up, it must also look like it holds something up. This "looking like," along with an idea of a history of building (or architecture) and a series of articulated formal rules, became what can be called architecture's "immanent metaphysic," its disciplinary core as well as its basic autonomy. Alberti's discourse was the first conscious human mediation to differentiate architecture from building, to see architecture as the sign of something as opposed to merely something.

This sign function, which distinguishes architecture from building, is central to the argument mandating a distinction between architecture and design. Pier Vittorio Aureli has argued that Alberti's discourse on architectural principles was a "way to establish architecture as a rational logical procedure irreducible to building." In these terms, architecture is something other than building, thus if building is the result of a "design" satisfying certain requirements for shelter, comfort, image, and meaning, then architecture is something other than design. This is not to say that there is no design in architecture, but rather that their objectives, and thus their resultant object, may be different. It is to the nature of that difference that the remainder of this essay will turn.

As design changed over time, so did architecture, specifically after the French Revolution, when the nature of both the subject and object change. The subject becomes a mass subject and the object is no longer a representation of divine power (will, intervention), or an individual secular or clerical ruler, but rather of the political and social will of the people. Thus, the principles that governed the idea of design would of necessity have to reflect this change. This is when design becomes something more than an aspect of painting.

With the new functions and new collective subject that were brought about after the French Revolution, the idea of design expanded. The idea of architecture set down by Alberti in the sixteenth century also was no longer adequate, hence the outpouring of French treatises in the early nineteenth century, in part to meet these new programmatic requirements. Thus, design and architecture could be said to be quite similar until the early part of the nineteenth century, when productivity linked to the mechanical revolution produced an expansion of capital, and with it, an excess of goods, the supply of which was greater than the demand. This created competition for new product, which nurtured the expansion of design into the production of objects and services that had not previously existed.

After World War II, as capital expanded and was invested in more aspects of consumer activity, design became increasingly more important. To grow the market required a continuous elaboration of new product to produce new markets. Media fueled the expansion of design through advertising. By now, architecture and design are no longer the same. Architecture is still an excess; it is not necessary, and therefore cannot be consumed as readily. Moreover, because it is an excess, it can already be critical; that is, it does not necessarily fulfill an objective but rather proposes alternatives. Thus, where today design has become unwittingly an agent of commodification, architecture has not.

Now, in 2010, in an age of shrinking economies in Western markets, seemingly two similar strategies for design and architecture are being followed. One is the pursuit of new, if not expanded, markets in Asia and other developing economies. The other is to suggest new products and new systems. Sustainability and the environment are two such tactics, but they merely increase the scope of the market. Architecture today is no more and no less necessary. It has always been sustainable, and importantly, through that sustainability, has contributed to the production of cultural artefacts. These cultural artefacts have traditionally resided in the world of symbols and icons; design artefacts, on the other hand, reside in the brand and are mostly devoid of such cultural iconicity.

This difference is sustained theoretically through the attitude of each discourse toward the hegemony of the metaphysical project. The basis for all metaphysics has been the possibility of meaning, whether in icons or symbols. While it can be argued that architecture will always mean, it is in no way a strong sign system. In fact, until recently, it was thought that architecture could be symbolic, rather than function as a sign, even though linguistic analogues, "architecture parlante," et cetera, have occupied much of architecture's theoretical expansion since the French Revolution.

Recent developments in post-structuralist thought have suggested the possibility that the sign/signified relationship once thought to be immutable could be broken apart. And since signs in architecture were in most cases the signified itself, that is, the column was also the sign of the column, architecture could now be thought to be moving from symbols to signs, and thence to the "becoming unmotivated of the sign." This leads to what Derrida calls the undecidability of the sign. It is here that the breach between design and architecture becomes a true rupture. While design is the creation of symbols and icons for clarity of meaning and, ultimately, for maintenance of the metaphysical project, for architecture today, it is the questioning of that very project that is at the core of its activity. This questioning ultimately leads to what can be called "disciplinary exceptions" revealed in the process. These exceptions become the self-critical matrix of differences that mark architecture. Design, in its drive for the normative or the standard, can never be that. The very term *architecture* carries the energy of that difference.

Spyros,

In the fall of 2008, you curated a lecture series on the theme of change, in which the introductory poster posed the question: "Is it possible to think of change as a dynamic process—a constantly evolving mechanism that includes accidents, periodic shifts, or even regressions to earlier paradigms?"

We at the Cornell Journal of Architecture *have been observing the language of change that has infiltrated the discipline of architecture, with terms such as* variation, biomorphism, *and* genetics. *However, change by itself is not enough: we assume that for meaningful change to occur, there must be an understanding and learning from a preexisting condition, based on feedback, analysis, and some form of repetition.*

What is the problem with change, and how can the perception of change be progressed?

—Eds.

Spyros Papapetros

is an assistant professor at the School of Architecture and the Program in Media and Modernity at Princeton University. His work focuses on the historiographies of art and architecture and the relationship between architecture, psychoanalysis, and psychological aesthetics.

Architecture and Regression

On the *Pre/post/erous* Histories of the Modern Movement

Perhaps the most pressing problem with change in recent architectural discussions is that our understanding of it has not changed at all. Once new styles or technologies replace older systems, they become as inflexible as their antecedents. Notions of historical progress, cultural transition, and social transformation appear as inert as the building structures that support (or oppose) such changes. Is it possible to think of change not as a static process, but as a dynamic one—a constantly evolving mechanism that includes accidents, periodic shifts, or even regressions to earlier paradigms? Predicated on a radical discontinuity with history, as well as a belief in technological progress, modern architecture and its militant historians have assigned notions of regression, repetition, and survival to the historicist mentality of the 19th century. However, the writings of modern architectural historians —from Giedion to Zevi, from Pevsner to Banham—are inundated with a set of revolving diagrams and spiraling correspondences with a broad range of historical eras. Antiquity, Renaissance and Baroque, or even the murkier areas of prehistory and the "immediate" (or distant) future, appear as pliable comparative models in which architectural modernity must perpetually re-inscribe its own historical position. But what happens during a period of radical transformation, such as the late 1960s, when notions of technological progress coexist with the ongoing crisis of the modern movement? What is the orientation that modern architecture must reflexively adopt when it implodes, and how can those retracing its trajectory reset its post-historical objectives?

Three

The year was 1967. Along with multimedia spectacles and phantasmagoric building structures, the euphoric technological environment of Montreal's Expo 67 hosted an international conference sponsored by the Noranda Mines Corporations and titled "Man and His World" ("Terre des Hommes"), also the general theme of the exposition. The long list of participants included a number of well-known scholars, such as the German philosopher Karl Löwith and the French paleoanthropologist André Leroi-Gourhan, as well as economists, politicians, physicists, astronomers, engineers, and medical researchers from four continents. The sole representative of architecture was the Italian critic and historian Bruno Zevi, who also participated at the exposition as a consultant for the Italian pavilion. The provocative title of Zevi's lecture, "Architecture 1967: Progress or Regression?" was drawn from a poignant association.[1] The "very happy event" of the Canadian centenary coincided with the third centenary of Carlo Borromini's suicide in 1667 (Zevi, "Progress" 175). One can imagine the silence in the audience following the historian's ominous comparison. It was as if the very scientific progress promoted by the seemingly unimpeded progress of the surrounding architecture had incited Zevi to revisit that "tragic episode" that had occurred exactly 300 years earlier. For the historian, the chronological correspondence signaled a more significant similarity in the circumstances surrounding the two different anniversaries. The Baroque master ended his life in total disillusionment after his innovative designs failed to be understood by his contemporaries. According to Zevi, Borromini's legacy mirrored that of Michelangelo, whose revolutionary architectural projects could only be properly understood four centuries after they were created, following the emergence of the modern movement. The radical innovations of Mannerist and Baroque architects were succeeded by a period that Zevi characterized as a "regression" to classical, more conventional models.

Transitioning from the Baroque to the contemporary, Zevi argued that in the wake of the architectural innovations of the first half of the 20th century, the modern movement was then facing a predicament similar to that of the classicist regression experienced in earlier historical periods. Some of the modern movement's original protagonists had recently died, and the survivors, though less suicidal (and less complex) than Borromini, partook in a professional behavior that was, Zevi implied, equally self-destructive. With the exception of Wright, who, like Borromini, maintained a standard of innovation throughout his multifaceted career, Zevi suggested that the postwar projects of modernist architects, including Gropius, Mies, or even the organicist Aalto, abandoned the anti-perspectivism and fluidity of their early projects in the 1920s and 1930s for the symmetrical facades and "boxy" monumentalism" of embassies, and office towers designed by the same architects throughout the 50s and 60s.

Bruno Zevi, "Historiographic and architectural rapport" between Francesco's Borromini's Sant'Ivo alla Sapienza in Rome and Frank Lloyd Wright's Guggenheim Museum in New York
from Archittetura e Storiografia: Le matrici antiche del linguaggio moderno (Turin: Einaudi, 1974). Courtesy of the Archive of the Bruno Zevi Foundation.

Only Le Corbusier (who had died less than two years earlier) was exempted from "the general rule of regression" by virtue of his abandonment of the "rationalism" of his early work in the 1920s for the "informal" architecture of Ronchamps and his other "gestural" postwar buildings (190).

For Zevi, the greatest problem in contemporary architecture was the emergence of an "architectural pluralism" fueled by an "eclecticist" approach that was purportedly "democratic," yet which at its core lacked "consistency" or commitment to any single ideology or formal principle. Here Zevi echoed some of the concerns voiced by Reyner Banham in his attack on the Italian Neo-Liberty movement (which the British historian diagnosed as a symptom of "infantile regression"), as well as by Nikolaus Pevsner in his 1961 RIBA lecture on the "return of historicism" in modern architecture.[2] If Banham criticized recent Italian architecture's regurgitation of the premodernist Art Nouveau, Pevsner lamented the modernist quotations in buildings by contemporary architects, who used the early 20th-century avant-gardes, from Expressionism to Functionalism, as an inventory of morphological precedents. Zevi's critique of pluralism also echoed the late writings of his rival Sigfried Giedion, who in the revised introduction to his *Space, Time, and Architecture* lamented the "playboy" attitude of contemporary architects that liberally shifted their formal repertoires and (non)critical positions from one project to the next.[3] Regressions followed progressions not in a rhythmic sequence, but according to a succession of circumstances. If progress was a straight line, regression was a wavering meander — a pliable trajectory that branched off into a plurality of meaningless digressions.

While Banham criticized Italian architects for their "Neo-Libertarian" ways, Zevi would single out a Scandinavian, Eero Saarinen, for his "pluralist" aberrations. Zevi disparaged Saarinen for meandering from the "romantic" character of the circular MIT chapel (1953) and the "Neo-medievalism" of the Yale student dormitories to the "structural" outlook of the Yale skating rink and the Dulles Airport, and then shifting once again to the expressionism of the TWA Terminal in New York (1956) (195). Zevi directed his most vehement invective against the recently completed Lincoln Center in New York—"what has been called 'the vanguard of crayfish,' that is, the vanguard of those who go backwards" (196).

Willemoesia, relative of crayfish from Demoor, Massart, and Vandervelde, *Evolution by Atrophy in Biology and Sociology* (New York: International Scientific Series, D. Appleton and Company, 1899).

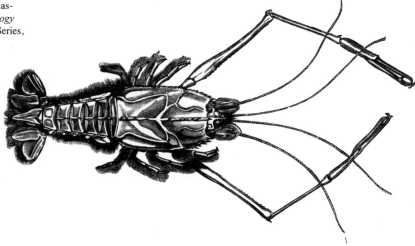

The biological metaphor discloses the evolutionary implications of Zevi's criticism of architectural regression. Like Wallace Harrison's glass curtain facade for the new Metropolitan Opera House (which echoed the "Pseudo-Venetian arches" of Edward Durrell-Stone that was also censured in Zevi's lecture), regression projects forward as a screen that covers a multitude of historical associations. Zevi envisions that historians examining the ruins of Lincoln Center 2,000 years later would find it hard to believe that it was constructed after the Bauhaus in Dessau or the Guggenheim Museum in New York; they would instead conclude that it was either a product of the late 18th century or an "offspring" of the 1893 Columbian exhibition (190). Here, the architectural historian projects two millennia forward and envisions himself as a future archaeologist who rediscovers the building and reclassifies it in its appropriate chronological order. Zevi undoes the architectural regression by a historiographic transgression. Modern architecture has to become a rudiment and regress into the status of prehistory in order to reclaim its true historical potential.

In his *Interpretation of Dreams*, Freud distinguishes between three kinds of regression in terms of its manifestation in dreams and neurotic symptoms. First, topographical regression: a state of antithetical orientation in the movement of psychic stimuli toward the perceptual end from which the latter have originated; second, temporal regression, which for Freud is "a harking back to older psychical structures" when mnemonic traces move toward earlier strata; and third, formal regression, in which "primitive methods of expression and representation take the place of the usual ones."[4] Freud's analysis of regression has both temporal and spatial implications. However, impossible as it might be to locate the position of memories, ideas, or thoughts in the psyche, what remains cogent is the notion of topographical orientation and temporal stratification in the arrangement of psychic properties that produce a series of expressive forms. The movement of regression cannot be limited to interior psychic regions, but must project to the external world. As Freud attests, the formal, temporal, and topographic aspects of regression "occur together as a rule;"[5] they produce a composite form that both regresses toward earlier interior strata and simultaneously progresses toward new modes of symbolic external expression.

In his 1967 lecture, Zevi not only speaks about regression, but he himself is also driven by it. It is as if the perceptual stimuli of the modern Expo reverberate with the memories of Baroque architectures, as well as a host of anxieties about the progress or decline of the modern movement. Central in every manifestation of regression is a notion of reverse orientation that unites origins with their (perceived) ends, thus creating a series of anachronic projections. The architectural historian becomes a pathologist who rediscovers symptoms of regression in formal resemblances and visual similarities, such as the ones invented in the histories constructed by Zevi and Giedion. History becomes the menacing object of historiography—either the recent history or the history that is morphologically closer to the present, and whose uncanny proximity makes it hard to bear.

Two

Anticipating Zevi's postapocalyptic scenarios, contemporary architecture itself had already turned into a form of prehistory clad by archaic, as well as futurist, patterns and associations. Toward the end of his Expo lecture, Zevi proclaimed that the legacy of the modern movement was "besieged by two opposing forces" (196) that had created a radical split. On one side was the academic "monumentalism" or "classicism" of high modernism, and on the other the "pop architecture" of Archigram—a "beat architecture" that lacked principles or "order of any kind," and which ultimately led into "chaos." Zevi dramatically concluded that the common objective of both of these camps "was to kill the modern movement and commit suicide" (196). If Borromini's suicide was for Zevi an act of redemption that could potentially salvage his own designs, as well as future architecture, then in contrast contemporary architects were driven by the intent to destroy everything that preceded them, including their own buildings. Acting as a psychopathologist, Zevi analyzed the modern movement as a formerly unified subject who now suffered from a personality split. In his well-known historiographic scheme, Zevi saw the development of architecture as a continuous spiral, a circuitous progression of architectural styles in which every phase is a necessary step toward the historical fulfillment of (organic) architecture.

Bruno Zevi, Diagram, from Storia dell' architettura moderna, 5th edition (Torino: Einaudi, 1975). Courtesy of the Archive of the Bruno Zevi Foundation.

While there were several opposing tendencies in the history of architecture—for example, functionalism and organicism, or functionalism and the romanticism of the 19th-century—movements would succeed one another without coinciding for a long period of time. The coexistence of two antithetical orientations was, for Zevi, a pathological symptom of the schizoid state of modern architecture and its endlessly bifurcating psychological vicissitudes.

In an attempt to escape the appalling "reality," as epitomized in the example of Lincoln Center, modern visionaries had regressed into "utopia," which now split into two more antithetical directions. Next to the impetuous drive toward the future, as displayed in the space-fiction iconography of the Archigram group, was a longing for the distant past and the origins of architecture in prehistory. Such tendencies instigated a return to the typology of the "cave"—an architecture "carved from inside," as evident in Frederick Kiesler's Endless House (which was exhibited in the late 1950s), as well as archaic and vernacular buildings. On one side of utopia orbited the interplanetary spacecrafts of the neofuturists celebrated by Banham, and on the other the hopeless neoromanticists that desired a return to the intrauterine environments of the surrealists or the circular abodes of tribal settlements. Included among such prized, ambiguously "prehistoric" specimens were the Dogon huts documented by Aldo Van Eyck, or the rock-cut dwellings in the south of France and Tunisia explored by the Smithsons, later to be retraced—in concrete—in their so-called House of the Future.[6]

It is here that we see how Zevi's dichotomy between "progress or regression" essentially collapsed. Since both orientations appeared to coexist, it could no longer be a matter of either/or. Like the time leap from the bone dangling ape-humans to the rotating space-stations in Stanley Kubrick's *2001: A Space Odyssey*,

 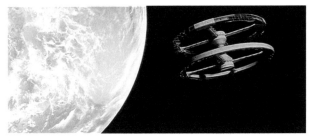

or the assemblage of fur-covered spaceships and pneumatic carriages driven by extraterrestrial cavemen in Rose Vandim's *Barbarella* (both films were released in 1968), prehistory acted as the backdrop for the delineation of futurist and/or eschatological visions. This incongruous mélange of both pre- and postapocalyptic landscapes would ultimately delineate a pre/post/erous history—a narrative that points to the origin and end of both humanity and (modern) architecture. Indeed, such anachronic narratives mark not only the end of modernism, but also the origin and brief life of what we call postmodern architecture.

It appears that at the beginning of the 1960s, architectural historians became obsessed not only with the decipherment of the past, but also the prognostication of the future. In his reflections on "the history of the immediate future," Banham envisioned the historian as a computer analyst, inserting all hard data from past histories and modern-day science to obtain a "graph" of future architectural developments.[7]

Historical interpretation was superseded by scientific projection and the desire to predict the future through both the present and the distant prehistoric past. However, prehistory offers no written records that could be processed as hard data by Banham's historiographic machine. Prehistory is susceptible to pliable interpretations and produces irregular "graphs" that are hard to either extend or interpret. It is the task of the historian, then, to fill the gaps of archaeological information with predictions, and to produce a future-anterior diagram of what it will have been. Zevi himself made similar predictions in the conclusion to his *Modern Language of Architecture*, titled "Prehistory and the Zero Degree of Architectural Culture."[8] Here, once again the Italian historian juxtaposed the neon signs of Las Vegas and the aesthetics of Pop Art with the "primitive elements of Paleolithic times" and the vernacular of "Architecture without Architects" (thus implicitly pitting the work of Robert Venturi and Denise Scott Brown against Bernard Rudofsky's MoMA exhibition) (Zevi, Modern Language, 221–222). Zevi's postscript was essentially a visual atlas of artfully arranged photographic collages that juxtaposed prehistoric, vernacular, and contemporary architectures, which were ingeniously choreographed with an acute sense of visual rhyming. For example, a full-page illustration combined photographic images of a Neolithic village in Northern Rhodesia, the pseudo-geodesic domes of "the hippy [*sic*] community of Drop City" in Trinidad, Colorado, and Moshe Safdie's Habitat,

Bruno Zevi, page with illustrations of Neolithic village in Northern Rhodesia, the pseudo-geodesic domes of "the hippy community of Drop City" in Trinidad, Colorado, and Moshe Safdie's Habitat from *Archittetura e Storiografia: Le matrici antiche del linguaggio moderno* (Turin: Einaudi, 1974). Courtesy of the Archive of the Bruno Zevi Foundation.

while the following page spread placed images of the craters of an underground community of "cavemen" in Tunisia next to Erich Mendelsohn's drawings of "the Architecture of the Dunes" (223–225). The final image sequence of the book was an aerial view of Stonehenge, preceded by a photograph of Pederson and Tilney's competition model for the Roosevelt Memorial in Washington, DC (1960), depicting "a crown of prehistoric stelae with platforms" (as Zevi noted in his caption), which was strongly reminiscent of the formal arrangement of the ancient site. The contemporary project follows Stonehenge, yet through its image precedes it. Even Zevi's illustration list reverses the sequence between pre and post.

Bruno Zevi, illustrations of William Pederson and Bradford Tilney competition model for the Roosevelt Memorial in Washington, DC (1960) and aerial view of "Temple of the Sun" at Stonehenge, from *Archittetura e Storiografia: Le matrici antiche del linguaggio moderno* (Turin: Einaudi, 1974). Courtesy of the Archive of the Bruno Zevi Foundation.

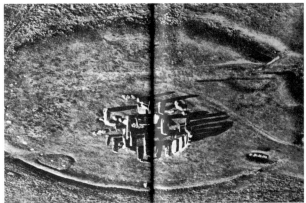

One

To be sure, prehistory has its own history in the annals of modern architecture. Preceding Zevi and contemporary with the practices of Kiesler and the Smithsons was Sigfried Giedion's research on prehistoric art and (to a lesser degree) architecture. Giedion's analyses were first presented in 1957 as a series of Mellon Lectures at the National Gallery in Washington, DC, and then later published as the first volume of his grand trilogy titled The Eternal Present.[9] Giedion's research was informed by the recent studies of paleoanthropologists such as Leroi-Gourhan and included visits to the original sites of Pech-Merle, Dordogne, and the Pyrenees. Using a number of formal principles—such as transparency and superimposition of shapes, lack of gravity and spatial orientation—Giedion linked prehistoric art with the work of 20th-century abstract painters such as Arp, Klee, Léger, and Picasso, concluding that prehistoric man (as Freud had already said) is really our contemporary. There can essentially be neither progress nor regression in the Eternal Present, for everything is projected and flattened onto the same plane. Unlike the linear "perspectival" development traced in *Space, Time and Architecture*, Giedion's later work presents a spiraling temporal system that allows the historian to expand the

trajectory of modern architecture from prehistory to the present, and to consolidate
its legacy in the future.

In the final part of his trilogy, *Architecture and the Phenomena of Transition*,
published posthumously, Giedion's "third space conception" began with modern
art and architecture in the early 20th century, synthesizing the previous two "space
conceptions," the first of which belonged to Egyptian (or Greek) and the second
to Roman antiquity. If the architecture of the first was a series of closed volumes,
such as the pyramids or Greek temples, from which space radiated outward, and
the architecture of the second was a lineage of grand structures, such as the Roman
Pantheon or other large public buildings, which were molded around a hollow
interior space, the architecture of the third space conception combined both of
these spatial attitudes in free volumes that comprised interpenetrating exterior and
interior spaces. Giedion's historiographic scheme amalgamates teleology with
posthistorical prognostication. If each of the previous historical space conceptions
had lasted for at least a couple of millennia, then the third one, that of modern architecture, was destined to live longer than its predecessors and, morever, to persist
eternally. In other words, modern architecture was here to stay: the 20th century
was "only the beginning."[10]

But one and two does not exactly make three, whether in the case of Giedion
or any other overarching post-Hegelian synthesis. By reflecting the skyscrapers
of New York onto Egyptian obelisks and pyramids, Giedion's third space conception was implicitly leading back toward the monolithic domain of the first. Bolder
in his eschatological predictions, Zevi decided to close his own account of modern
architecture not with the number three, but with the "degree zero," the level of
prehistory—not as a nihilistic or impossible utopia, but as a nondirectional space
of infinite possibilities.

Zero

Often in such spiraling (pre)histories, a distant origin merges with an "end"
that has already occurred or it is imminent. As becomes evident in Bataille's essays
on prehistoric art, most of them dating from the 1940s and 1950s, the contemporary
resurgence of interest in prehistory was instigated by the momentous discovery
of the cave paintings of Lascaux and other sites and objects from the Paleolithic
era, yet was inevitably tinged by the horrors of the war, including Auschwitz and
Hiroshima.[11] Speaking before Zevi in the 1967 "Man and His World" conference in
Montreal, Karl Löwith discussed scientific "progress" as a form of "fatality" often
related to "destruction."[12] The philosopher mentioned the role of science in the
creation of nuclear weapons and the misuse of atomic energy in the World War II
(*Man and His World*, 93). In the beginning of his lecture on "The land of prehistoric
men" (which preceded the talks by Löwith and Zevi in the same conference), the
paleoanthropologist Leroi-Gourhan made a similarly ominous historical comparison, by reminding his audience that in the Middle Ages, prehistoric remains, such
as "heaps of sea-shells or enormous bones" would "testify to the material reality of
the Deluge (71)."[13] Prehistoric specimens not only announced but were re-created
by echoes of the deluge. The catastrophic impact of the World War II had rendered
everything that preceded it into a form of prehistory: dark, unknowable, murky.

All objects, starting with buildings, had to be reinvented by starting from "degree zero"—the flatness of the prehistorical desert. Postwar prehistories were (mal) formed by the insecurities of a postnuclear condition that gave birth to both eschatological and cosmogonic visions—fantasies of an originary prehistory that could absolve the future by the ambient properties of a virtual past. Similar to Zevi's projection of Lincoln Center as a quasi-post-apocalyptic "ruin," the objects of modern architecture were now rediscovered as the fossils of an unlocatable prehistory, their own origin and end becoming part of a (post)historical prediction.

But let us now close by regressing to Zevi's "crayfish" reference in his description of the pre/post/erous rudiments of Lincoln Center. Toward the turn of the previous century, a group of Belgian natural theorists and sociologists published a book on the idea of "regressive evolution"—a supplement to, as well as critique of, Darwin's earlier theories. According to the Belgian scientists, every (r)evolution is preceded by a form of devolution. No progress can ever occur without regression; no forward movement can take place without recoil. In order to gain one thing, an organism has to lose something else.[14] The processes of degeneration and atrophy were essential to the continuation of life, and so too were organic rudiments and relics. Could discourses of regression and prehistoric origins in architecture, then, have a similarly regenerative function? Could the very invocation of the prehistoric caves or the Borrominian Baroque create new alliances between post and past architectures and delineate historical correspondences with the present? Could the transformation of contemporary buildings into relics, such as the premature ruination of Lincoln Center catalyzed by Zevi, in fact, propel the posthumous evolution of modern architecture? Departing from the linear progress of Renaissance and Classical architectural discourses and from the radical discontinuity of historical process espoused by the modern movement, recent architectural culture advances another model of history—that of regression, temporal revolution, and spiraling anachronism. By turning back or looking back at itself from a distance, architectural history reinstates its critical dimension through a series of projective historiographic operations. Regression, regurgitation of earlier materials, recurrence, or return, are not simply traumatic repetitions of a past that is essentially unknowable, but are also sources of renewal for a disciplinary orthodoxy that has become stale.

Endnotes

1 Bruno Zevi, "Architecture 1967: Progress or Regression?" in *Man and His World (Terre des Hommes): The Noranda Lectures Expo 67*, Helen S. Hogg (ed.) (Toronto: University of Toronto Press, 1968), 173–200.

2 Banham Reyner, "Neo-Liberty: The Italian Retreat from Modern Architecture," in *The Architectural Review* 125 (April 1959), 230–235; and Nikolaus Pevsner "Modern Architecture and the Historian or the Return of Historicism," *RIBA Journal* 68 (April 1961), 230–242.

3 Sigfried Giedion, "Introduction—Architecture in the 1960s: Hopes and Fears," in *Space Time and Architecture*, 5th rev. ed. (Cambridge, MA: Harvard University Press, 1967), xxxii.

4 Sigmund Freud, *The Interpretation of Dreams* (1900), in *The Standard Edition of the Complete Psychological Works of Sigmund Freud*, vol. 5, James Strachey (trans.) (London: The Hogarth Press, 1955), 547.

5 Freud, *The Interpretation of Dreams*, p. 547.

6 On the iconography of the Smithsons's House of the Future, see Beatriz Colomina, "Unbreathed Air 1956," *Grey Room*, no. 15 (Spring 2004), 28–59.

7 Reyner Banham, "The History of the Immediate Future," *RIBA Journal* 68 (May 1961), 252–260, 269.

8 Bruno Zevi, *The Modern Language of Architecture* (Seattle: University of Washington Press, 1978), 218–233. See also Bruno Zevi, *Il linguaggio moderno dell'architettura* (Turin: Einaudi, 1973) and *Archittetura e Storiografia: Le matrici antiche del linguaggio moderno* (Turin: Einaudi, 1974).

9   Sigfried Giedion, *The Eternal Present Volume I: The Beginnings of Art* (New York: Bollingen Foundation and Pantheon Books, 1962). As mentioned in the acknowledgments in his book, Giedion had delivered several other lectures on prehistoric art, starting with a lecture titled "Prehistoric and Contemporary Means of Artistic Expression," delivered in the International Congress for Prehistoric and Protohistoric Sciences in Zurich in 1950. Giedion, *The Eternal Present*, ix.

10 Sigfried Giedion, *Architecture and the Phenomena of Transition* (Cambridge, MA: Harvard University Press, 1971).

11 See, for example, his "Notes for a Film," in George Bataille, *The Cradle of Humanity: Prehistoric Art and Culture*, Stuart Kendall (ed. and trans.) (New York: Zone Books, 2005), 179–185.

12 Karl Löwith, "Progress: A Fatality," in *Man and His World* (see note 1), 81–95.

13 André Leroi-Gourhan, "Terre des hommes préhistoriques," in *Man and His World* (see note 1), 71–80.

14 Jean Demoor, Jean Massart, and Émile Vandervelde, *L'évolution regressive en biologie et sociologie* (Paris: Alcan, 1897). English edition: *Evolution by Atrophy in Biology and Sociology*, Chalmers Mitchell (trans.) (New York: International Scientific Series, D. Appleton and Company, 1899).

From: The *Cornell Journal of Architecture* (cjoa@cornell.edu)
Sent: Dec. 12, 2009 6:03 p.m.
To: Greg.Lynn@aud.ucla.edu
Subject: RE

Dear Greg,
The discipline is turning more and more toward biomimetic morphogenetic strategies for its language, a language that you must take some responsibility for propagating. Yet your points of departure (at least, in Folds, Bodies & Blobs*) were often architectural references, from Palladio to Rowe to Eisenman. The* Cornell Journal of Architecture 8: RE *invites you to write on the role of architectural feedback and mull the question of whether or not intelligent systems can be operative and performative while still looping through architectural precedent.*

Issue 8 moves away from the idea of a single-themed issue toward a new conceptualization of the Journal *as a location for evolving critical dialogue.* RE *embodies the essence of this strategy.*

In addition to being the chemical symbol for rhenium, the symbol for the rupee, a musical variant spelling of ray, and many abbreviations, RE *has two major uses: (1) meaning with regard to, as the preposition in contexts such as re: your letter; and (2) as the prefix indicating return to a previous condition, as in review, reiterate, resume, reimagine, react, redo, and so on. Both uses suggest dialogue, criticism, feedback, and testing of an existing condition: a text, a building, a methodology.*

Please consider this. It would be a key article for us, and we think it might be interesting for you too. Details are attached.
—Eds.

Greg Lynn

*is presently an o. Univ. Prof. Arch. at angewandte Vienna, UCLA,
and Yale University. He was the recipient of the Golden Lion at
the 2009 Venice Biennale of Architecture and is a member of the
Academy of Arts and Letters.*

Thanks,
but No Thanks

From: Greg.Lynn@aud.ucla.edu
Sent: Dec. 12, 2009 6:47 p.m.
To: The *Cornell Journal of Architecture* (cjoa@cornell.edu)
RE: RE

Thanks for the invite *Cornell Journal of Architecture,*

I am afraid that I can't take on any new writing deadlines at this time or else I would
do it in a minute. It is a topic that I would enjoy writing about, as the substitution of
the internet for books and libraries has equaled a loss of anything with deeper historic
relevance than a newsfeed or press release. Architectural precedents and design
discourse is virtually unknown to today's students. I feel lucky to have experienced
the dialogue between designers and scholars through international conferences,
scholarly magazines, and provocative exhibitions. This is one way to evaluate
design innovation and quality. Conspiring with the absence of this kind of design
discourse is the practice of analyzing extra-architectural statistics and other data
for the pseudo-scientific justification for design decisions. This cynically erases the
need for disciplinary knowledge, reflection, and discussion. I find it a very disturbing
moment in the field and at the schools. Software has something to do with it but
little when compared to the vacuum of disciplinary awareness and the celebration of
clever shallow trickery mostly emanating from The Netherlands in the 90s. Sadly, this
is all I can write on the topic as I am far behind on other texts I have already made
commitments to write. Good luck with the issue, it should be great. I like the topic
very much.

Best,
Greg